SIGN LANGUAGE MADE SIMPLE

Edgar D. Lawrence

Graphic Design / Mike Johnson

Gospel Publishing House
Springfield, Missouri

02—0604

Dedicated to the Memory of

Alan Terpening
1952 - 1974

He is affectionately
remembered as director of the
Living Signs Choir
(Central Bible College),
as an interpreter, a friend, and
a Christian
whose total dedication
to the ministry to the deaf
left a lasting impression on all
who knew him.

©1975 by
Gospel Publishing House
Springfield, Missouri 65802.

ISBN 0-88243-604-X

Library of Congress
Catalog Card Number: LCC-75-20740

Printed in the United States of America

Contents

Acknowledgments

Particular mention and appreciation is due to many people who helped make this book a reality. Jacob Trout, Eldon Post, and Jeanne Manning offered encouragement and professional consultation; Edward and Charlotte Graham read the proofs of the original lessons that make up this book; Mike Johnson handled the design/art responsibilities; Richard Slaton served as production artist; the Board of Administration and students of Central Bible College assisted in getting the lessons into print; Jack Green, a friend of many years, provided the sketch of Alan Terpening; David J. Johnston and Wayne Warner of the Gospel Publishing House guided this work through the production stages.

A book of this nature obviously represents endless hours of work—hours that were taken from my normal family activities. Therefore, I offer a special word of appreciation to my wife Delna; and children, Jim, Starla, Paul, and Rhonda.

Edgar D. Lawrence

Introduction

The book you are about to use is designed so you can learn the language of signs in the easiest, fastest, and most practical method—enabling you to communicate with the deaf almost immediately.

Over a period of several years, parents, relatives, and others interested in communicating with the deaf have requested a simple yet thorough book which they could use to learn the sign language. I believe this total communication book will meet that need as well as give students a visual pattern with which to practice outside the classroom.

The 600 sentences which make up the 30 lessons have been used in a classroom setting since 1968, with the instructor demonstrating the signs. The inspiration to place these sentences in graphic art came from watching my preschool children sign stories that had been portrayed in signed English. It seemed reasonable that if children could learn the language of signs by looking at pictures, surely adults could do the same.

The vocabulary introduced in the first few lessons deals with common, everyday expressions such as "Hello," "How are you?" "I am fine," etc. As you progress in the lessons, you will expand your vocabulary and review what you have already learned.

Do not become discouraged if the movements are not as smooth as you wish at first. Practice is the key. The signed sentences in this book should be practiced a minimum of three times weekly. Learning any language requires practice, and anyone who fails to practice will make little progress.

The fingerspelling drills should be practiced until the hand configuration becomes so familiar to the eye that it is recognized instantly. Do not fingerspell the words slowly because it will defeat the purpose of the drills. The same applies to signed numbers.

Fingerspelling of the whole alphabet is discouraged. Spell words instead. When "reading" fingerspelling, do so phonetically as it is spelled. Although you may mispronounce the word, you will have the spelling in mind.

Religious signs are emphasized in the last few lessons to make this book useful in both secular and religious settings. The Bible passages and religious choruses in the appendix are excellent for learning fluency of signs, smoothness, and beauty in form. All Scripture portions and choruses are numbered to correlate with the lessons. The vocabulary of the Scripture portions and choruses is included in the lessons.

The author holds no claim as the final authority on how a specific word is signed, but it was necessary to settle on one sign for each word in the 30 lessons. As you become familiar with communicating with the deaf, you will learn other signs for the same words. Colloquial signs often differ from the ones illustrated in this book. However, you will be able to easily adapt to the sign used in the area where you live. Learn as many of the variations as possible to give yourself a wider range in communicating with the deaf.

The artist shows the various signs from different angles and with movement not always in the same direction. This is to show the clearest view possible for your immediate understanding.

Learning to sign is but 50 percent of communication. You must practice reading the signs of the deaf. Use facial expressions, gestures, and even pantomine to communicate—but communicate. When communicating with the deaf or hard-of-hearing person, speak your sentences aloud as you sign. This will give him opportunity to use what hearing ability he does have; and, too, the deaf depend on lip movement to recognize the synonyms used in a sentence.

Now you are ready to learn total communication skills, a system that will enable you to communicate with some of the more than 13 million deaf and the hearing — impaired in the United States.

May your study of the sign language be a happy and rewarding experience.

Edgar D. Lawrence

History
of the Sign Language

The language of signs is ancient. Since earliest recorded history, gestures have been used for communication between groups of dissimilar languages and cultures. The development of formal signs, however, has been slow, with the first attempt to do so occurring in the latter part of the 16th century.

Until the 16th century, it was considered futile to attempt to educate the deaf. They were scorned, reviled, ridiculed, and even feared. They were thought to be incapable of reasoning, thinking, or having ideas.

During the 16th century an Italian physician, Girolamo Cardano, felt that the hearing of words was not needed for the understanding of ideas, so he developed a code for teaching the deaf. Although his code was never used, his ideas, however, prepared the way for changing the attitude that the deaf were unable to learn.

It was in Spain that the first successful attempts to educate the deaf were made. A Spanish Monk, Pedro Ponce de Leon, succeeded in educating the deaf children of several noble Spanish families so that they were declared legally qualified to inherit their families' estates. Apparently, Ponce de Leon taught these children to read and write and later to speak.

Still later, Juan Martin Pablo Bonet wrote a book on the education of the deaf. He advocated teaching a one-handed manual alphabet as the first step in educating the deaf child. This manual alphabet is essentially the same as is used today.

Public education of the deaf began in France and Germany. It was also in those countries that the "methods" argument began. In France, Abbe Charles de l'Epee founded the first public school for the deaf. Besides being considered the father of public education for the deaf, he is also considered the father of the language of signs.

Abbé de l'Epée believed that the language of signs was the natural language of the deaf people and that their education should be based on it. But he also recognized that the primitive signs used by deaf people of that day were too rudimentary to be used as an educational tool, so he gave himself to refining and developing this language of signs into a full language. Our present-day sign language is based upon his system.

In Germany, however, Samuel Heinicke was originating what eventually came to be known as the German method. In brief, it was the oral method of teaching a deaf child through speech and speechreading, with sign language absolutely forbidden. This started a controversy that persists somewhat to this day. However, recent research projects have statistically proved Total Communication to be of the greatest advantage to the deaf.

Thomas Hopkins Gallaudet was a minister. He became the developer of American Education of the deaf, founder of the first school for the deaf in this country and the man for whom Gallaudet College, the only liberal arts college for the deaf in the world, was named.

Gallaudet was approached by Dr. Mason Cogswell, who had a deaf daughter, Alice. Dr. Cogswell asked Gallaudet to journey to Europe and study the methods developed there to teach the deaf. He journeyed to England first to study their methods, meaning to combine the best of both methods, oral and manual, but this was unacceptable to the English educators he contacted. They wished him to use only their methods. About this time, Abbe Sicard arrived on a lecture tour in London with two of his most famous pupils. Gallaudet was so impressed by the demonstrations that he abandoned his negotiations with the English and went to Paris to study with Sicard.

After studying with Sicard for a few months, Gallaudet returned to America, bringing with him Laurent Clerc, who became the first deaf teacher of the deaf in the United States. Together, they founded the American Asylum for the Deaf and Dumb in Hartford, Connecticut, the present American School for the Deaf.

From this beginning, sign language became the national language for the deaf in America. It has been developed and refined until it is now a classical and beautiful--and also picturesque--language of gesture by which the great majority of the deaf communicate with each other--and with their hearing friends who take the trouble to learn the language of signs.

It is idiomatic, it incorporates pantomimes, it is individualistic and sometimes confusing to a beginner. But it is always interesting, and a student of the language of signs will find it greatly rewarding as he progresses to better communication with his deaf friends. And such student, if he persists can eventually become so fluent that he can help his deaf compatriots in one of the most vital ways a hearing person can help the deaf — by becoming an interpreter, and opening the door for the deaf to gain insight into what goes on in the sometimes baffling world of the hearing.*

A more recent development in communication with the deaf is what is called, "Total Communication." It is the author's opinion that anyone learning the language of signs should be cognizant of this system; hence attention is drawn to the following article by Dr. Denton regarding "Total Communication."

* Barbara E. Brasel, **An Introductory Course in Manual Communication.**

The Philosophical Basis for
Total Communication

David M. Denton, Ph.D., Superintendent of the Maryland School for the
Deaf and Recipient of the 1972 Dan Cloud Leadership Award

Introduction

Education should be concerned with the very essence of
existence itself, with being, and learning, and living and doing.
An educational philosophy then should embrace all areas of the
individual's development and should encompass the whole
spectrum of life experiences. Too frequently, educational
philosophies address themselves to instructional methods and
courses of study. There is more, however, to living than being
instructed in a certain manner, using certain instructional
methods, and in certain predetermined areas of interest.

In my opinion, an educational philosophy would concern itself
with the long-term goals that society has established for its
members; that is, a sensitivity to the needs of other people, an
attitude of responsible service to these needs, intellectual
awareness of alternatives, and the ability to choose an
appropriate response or action. In my opinion, an educational
philosophy should rest upon a foundation of moral and spiritual
principles; principles which transcend religious or ethnic
differences and make possible directed purposeful, meaningful
human existence.

To be valid, an educational philosophy must be based upon
an understanding of the learning process. Of equal importance
is the realization that most learning occurs through interaction
with other people and that such interaction is possible only
under conditions where persons are able to communicate with
understanding. This is of overwhelming importance where
persons with communication disability are concerned.

Speech given at the Annual Dan Cloud Memorial Award Program at
California State University, Northridge, August 2, 1972. Used by
permission.

Total Communication — The Parents and The Infant

For a century and a half, the formal education of many deaf children has been initiated at 5 or 6 upon entrance into an educational program, but without the benefit of those five or six years of cumulative learning that occur naturally for the hearing child, who functions as a participating member of a social institution, within an environment which is understood and acted upon by the individual child. The deaf child has been **within an environment, but not a part of it.** His relationship to the environment is not understood and even more importantly, his relationship with the other persons in the environment is not understood. As a result, the child, of course, cannot have a true sense of identity. Piaget, the noted child psychologist and etymologist, has said "Learning is possible only when there is active assimilation... Knowledge is not a copy of reality. To know an object, to know an event, is not simply to look at it, and make a mental copy or image of it. To know an object is to act on it. To know is to modify, to transform the object, and to understand the process of this transformation, and as a consequence, to understand the way the object is constructed. An operation is thus the essence of knowledge; it is an interiorized action which modifies the object of Knowledge." Keep this in mind, it will be referred to later in the discussion of the linguistic process.

In the meantime, let us consider the deaf infant and his relationship with his parents and other members of the family. The importance of what Piaget has said is readily apparent when we consider the tenuous relationships of the young deaf child with the other members of his social, cultural world.

The realization of one's own existence is possible only in terms of one's relationship with other people. One's identity, then, is measured in terms of his role among those persons within the immediate environment. The child's role within the family, then, is of major importance. This role emerges and develops from infancy and is initially based upon the child's relationship with his mother and father. We cannot expect the deaf child to postpone **becoming a person** until he has reached school age or even preschool age and has **begun** to learn to communicate. The fact of the matter is that his personality will reflect his barrenness, the emptiness, the uncertainty, and the superficiality of his relationship with parents with whom he is unable to communicate. It is not uncommon to find young deaf men and women of college age, who have grown up within a home, but who are without an understanding of the social, cultural, religious, political views, and attitudes of their own families. Under such conditions or circumstances, the deaf child is left to develop his self concept and his personality within a relative vacuum as far as social, cultural, oral, scriptural influences are concerned. Deaf children cannot be abandoned to drift on a sea of uncertain choices.

The quality of the relationship between a child and his parents is based upon the level and the quality of communication existing between them. The deaf child is entitled to a relationship of understanding and trust with his parents and members of the family at **all levels of his development**... not just when he has acquired the tools for communication.

If oral only communication was adequate for the purpose of developing the kind of relationship between deaf child and parent that is essential for normal psycho-social development, then this discussion would be unnecessary. Similarly, if oral only communication between parent and deaf child was adequate for the purpose of leading the deaf child toward competence in language, then there would be no need for this presentation on something called Total Communication. Limitation of communication between parent and deaf child to oral means only, serves not only to restrict linguistic development, but operates as well as a denial of the deaf child's **right to be.** To repeat, the deaf child grows toward self-realization only when he is able to function with a feeling of self worth and as a contributing, sharing member of the family. Total Communication, then, operates as an **affirmation** of the child's **right to be.** Those very, very fundamental attitudes, feelings, concepts can be expressed by the mother of a deaf infant using **signs** to accompany spoken words. Since these signs are not only graphically dramatic and large enough for the infant to see without difficulty, but **concept based** as well, they provide the tool for initial linguistic interaction between the parent and child. The deaf infant is entitled to the right to share the traditional bedtime stories and nursery rhymes, children's prayers that any other child enjoys. This entitlement can be realized only through the use of a total, oral, manual, auditory system of communication. For parents of a deaf infant who actively employ a Total Communication system within the home, two critically important goals can be achieved.

First of all, it is possible to develop between and among the parents and the deaf child, a relationship of genuine acceptance and understanding that will foster optimum psycho-social development. Secondly, through early introduction to a stable symbol system the deaf child will be able to develop linguistically on the strength of his ability to interact with other members of the family. Here the **self-generating** quality of language comes into play.

Total Communication — The Linguistic Process

For far too many years, the education of the deaf has poured much of its energy into the **teaching of language**. Various methods have been developed which allegedly enhance the teaching of language. Various teaching tools such as the Fitzgerald Key, Wings Symbols, and the Barry Five Slate Method have been developed and used to help deaf children more **clearly see the structure of language**. Therein, perhaps, lies much of the whole problem. **Seeing the structure of language** is not nearly so important as **feeling the structure of language**. Language, then, is an interiorized process. This, I believe, is what Piaget was talking about, if you will recall his statements which I read a few moments ago. By age 6, a hearing child, of normal intelligence, knows practically all the essential grammatical structures of his language. All of this language know-how is acquired without formal teaching or structuring or programming. The secret ingredient is "functional communication." Children learn to understand and use language to serve themselves as they operate on the environs of their social-cultural world. We are now beginning to appreciate the fact that the deaf child learns language under the same conditions and according to the same developmental sequence as does the hearing child. Briefly, the deaf child must be free to interact and experiment with a reliable symbol system, find out for himself how it works, and continue to expand it through usage. Linguistic development occurs then on the basis of what we might call an "interactional model" for both the deaf child and the hearing child. In a nutshell, the interactional model would mean that language **naturally** develops out of **meaningful dialogue.**

After the child has acquired a symbol which he can use, he then begins to generate language through experimentation. Since language is self-expanding, through usage, then enrichment can go on wherever the child happens to be -- at home, in school, in the dormitory, or on the playground. It is, of course, essential that the adults in each of these environments reflect back to the child the language he needs to use.

On the basis of demonstrated needs, the Maryland School for the Deaf formally adopted four years ago, the philosophy of Total Communication to serve all educable children with a severe to profound hearing impairment. **For this purpose Total Communication is defined as the right of every deaf child to learn to use all forms of communication so that he may have the full opportunity to develop language competence at the earliest possible age. This implies introduction to a reliable, receptive-expressive symbol system in the preschool years between birth and age 5. Total Communication includes the full spectrum of language models: child devised gestures, the language of signs, speech, speechreading, fingerspelling, reading, and writing. Total Communication also holds that every deaf child should have the opportunity to develop any remnant of residual hearing for the enhancement of speech and speechreading skills through the use of individual and/or high fidelity group amplification system.** We at the Maryland School for the Deaf feel a great need to document Total Communication and to refine the concepts as we understand them more clearly. At the present time, the School is involved with Dr. Donald F. Moores from the University of Minnesota in a research project relating to communication methods. The School is also involved with Dr. McCay Vernon and Dr. Earl Griswold of Western Maryland College in the development of films based upon the concept of Total Communication. Further, the School is involved in the development of a communication profile on every student enrolled. This is being done with the help of Dr. Donald Johnson of the National Technical Institute for the Deaf.

We have attempted to translate in the form of a diagram, the Total Communication concept of language development in the very young child with profound hearing impairment from birth. We refer to this diagram as the "Communication Keystone." This name seems appropriate both in terms of its geometric shape and in terms of its symbolic meaning, as binding together the parts of the communication process, into a meaningful whole.

HIERARCHY OF COMMUNICATION FOR THE CONGENITALLY DEAF CHILD

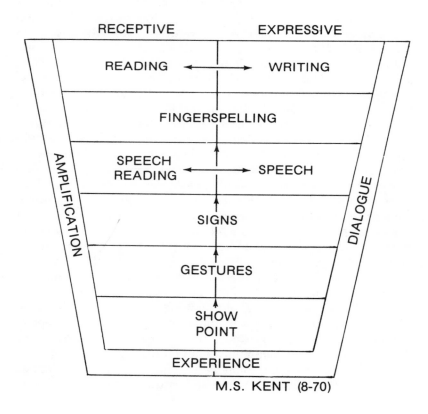

M.S. KENT (8-70)

Based upon our experience with Total Communication, we are prepared to make the following statement:

1. Signs are the easiest means of getting the very young congenitally deaf to communicate in the true sense of the word, that is to express his own ideas. When this happens, we see positive changes in behavior and an improvement in interpersonal relationships. The deaf child joins the family as a fully participating member.

2. Signs reinforce speechreading and audition when the adult (teacher, parent, houseparent) signs and talks simultaneously and the child is using amplification adequate for his needs. For the child who cannot benefit from amplification (very few in number), signs reinforce speechreading. Speech for this child must be developed purely on a kinesthetic basis. Language development, however, is not tied to his progress in speech.
   When speech and signs are practiced simultaneously, acceptable syntactic structure is more apt to occur. This is usually the way the hearing person learns to associate signs with words. The combination of speech and signs provides a syntactical model for the deaf child to imitate, both visually and auditorially. When a deaf adult uses speech with signs, he consciously organizes his signing syntactically. Consequently, deaf persons improve their oral skills and hearing persons improve their manual skills. The result is better communication on both sides.

3. Audition (High Gain Amplification) reinforces aural-oral skills (Speech and Speechreading) for many deaf children when the equipment is of a quality to reach the hearing impairment. Success in this area is dependent upon auditory feedback or the degree to which the child can hear his own as well as the speech of others.

4. Fingerspelling reinforces reading and writing. Fingerspelling requires a similar level of maturation and background of language experience as reading and writing. We do not consider it any more practical to start the preschool deaf child with fingerspelling than we do to start the hearing preschool child's language development with reading and writing. Signs provide the "coin to exchange" for transmission of ideas and for the generation of syntax at an early age.

We are beginning to see dramatic changes among our upper-primary students who are 9, 10, and 11 years of age. Most of these students have now had two or three years of a Total Communication Program. Traditionally, reading comprehension levels of this age group have been around second grade and we had to settle for increments of a half grade or a .5 gain per year. In this group of approximately 40 students, we are seeing many more children achieve a reading comprehension level greater than 2.5 grade levels. Almost two-thirds or 61 percent of this group scored higher than 2.5 in reading comprehension on the May 1971 achievement tests. These students were measured on the Gates MacGinitie Reading Tests. Even more interesting perhaps is the observation that 46 percent of this group scored 3.0 or better, while 23 per cent scored 3.5 or better and 10 percent scored above 4.0.

Increment from September 1970 to May 1971 was equally heartening. Nearly one half of this group or 43 percent made at least a full grade level gain. This is much higher than we had anticipated. We attribute much of this growth to... better communication on all sides... exchange of ideas, etc., but more basically, to signs which serve as the building blocks upon which the congenitally deaf child can develop his own linguistic base.

We are finding that the knowledge of signs spills over into speech and speechreading as well as syntax. A recent classroom incident illustrates the positive influence of manual communication on speech production of young profoundly deaf children. While visiting a class of primary children recently, a 7-year-old girl approached me and told me that she would like to do a poem for me. The teacher told her to go ahead and do the poem, but to remember the final "g" sound in the word flag and final "d" sound in the word red. The child smiled and indicated that she would try to remember these sounds. She then turned to me and signed and said simultaneously: "We love our flag" (as she signed flag she ended the graceful movement of her right hand by assuming the g formation. This act seemed to provide the visual as well as the kinesthetic monitoring for her own speech production and she was able to produce a very good g sound), "of red and white and blue." As this young girl signed and said the word red, her index finger moved downward and outward from her lips and her right hand assumed formation d of the manual alphabet. Again, being able to use her hands seemed to provide her with the necessary feedback to aid in the development of the rather difficult **d** sound. Of course, not to be overlooked is the fact that this little child did this whole poem using Total Communication and with full understanding of the meaning of the poem itself.

In considering the above statements, keep in mind the fact that the key to this kind of program is the unstructured, randomized, but highly personalized and therefore relevant dialogue between child and adult and child and child.

Total Communication — The Spiritual Dimension

If we are able to fully embrace the philosophy of Total Communication, then we must recognize that all dimensions of the deaf child's existence must be considered -- including the spiritual dimension. I am deeply concerned about what I consider to be one of the most neglected areas in the lives of so many of our deaf citizens, including both children and adults. Sometimes it seems that we, as professional people, become so engrossed in the other dimensions of a deaf person's existence that religious or spiritual development is given extremely low priority or is completely forgotten. More, not less, effort is required in meeting the spiritual needs of deaf children and adults than is true of hearing people. This relates, of course, to the problem of communication. Those basic, but not so important spiritual, moral, and religious concepts and principles must be introduced early into the life of a deaf child, and this, of course, must be done in a way that is understandable and useful by the child himself. Relevance and personal involvement in the spiritual area is as important as it is in the academic area. Basic to this, of course, is the obvious fact that the family must be able to provide a personal, spiritual involvement for the deaf member of the family. Perhaps this should be a part of parent counseling while the child is still young.

Before going further, let me identify for you what I consider to be three major problem areas in existing religious services and programs for deaf people. These problem areas involve what we could term Quantity, Quality, and Style. The first and most obvious deals with the number of religious programs available for deaf people. The problem is that too few churches on a national and local level provide a program for religious involvement for deaf persons. The need, of course, is for a new level of sensitivity and responsiveness on the part of organized religious groups to fully embrace and totally involve deaf people as active and responsive members of the church congregation. The second deals with the quality of many existing religious services for the deaf. Too many of them still continue to institutionalize deaf worshipers by separating them into a special group, or by providing opportunities for participation in only part of the total worship experience. Far too frequently the membership of a local church is aware only of the physical interaction. It is almost as if the deaf persons were considered non-persons. Perhaps we need to be jolted into a realization that deaf people, not only have something to get from the worship, but they also have much to give.

Number three deals with the style or pattern of typical church programs for the deaf. They tend to follow the pattern of passive or spectator type of participation rather than personal involvement. Someone interpreting a sermon is much better than nothing, but is it adequate to bring the deaf members into full spiritual fellowship? Another characteristic of traditional programs is that they tend to group deaf persons of all ages together and treat them as a single group, with a single need. Churches must begin to minister to deaf persons of all ages from nursery school onward. Whatever a church provides the regular membership should also be made available to the deaf. To consider the concept of education or rehabilitation without considering man's spiritual dimension, is to deny one of the fundamental truths of human existence. Perhaps it seems strange that I, as an educator, am standing before you talking about spiritual development of deaf people. Perhaps it is strange, but I feel very strongly that if we do not first **look to ourselves** for leadership, then to whom do we look? If asked what my biggest concern for the future was, I would have to answer that it involves the growing insensitivity to the need for nurturing our children's spiritual lives and the seeming unwillingness of our social institutions to provide children with a set of moral, spiritual values sufficient to sustain them during times of personal crisis and sufficient to prepare them for lives of responsible service to the other people. I am not talking about the doctrinal nor theological aspects of religion, but rather of the recognition that deaf people do have souls.

Total Communication — The School's Commitment

When the Maryland School for the Deaf embraced the philosophy of Total Communication four years ago, it also embraced a whole set of new responsibilities.

First among these was a recognition that the School could not function in isolation and, of necessity, must involve itself with, first of all, the parents of the children enrolled, and secondly with the adult deaf community. This is based upon the belief that education does not and cannot exist separate and apart from home and the community, regardless of how excellent the established educational program is. It could almost be said that the School is an extension of the family and the community. Over the past three years, the Maryland School of the Deaf has established and maintained Parent Communication Classes all over the State of Maryland. During the Spring semester of 1972, the School directly supported 12 such classes and was involved in a number of others. During this three-year period, staff members from the School have driven in excess of 100,000 miles, **at night without pay**, staffing these classes. This will provide you with some evidence of the level and the quality of the commitment of our wonderful staff. Response from our parents has been unusually enthusiastic. We have yet to encounter any organized resistance to our Total Communication Program from parents anywhere within the state.

At the time Total Communication was adopted by the School, we found that the communication skills of all of our personnel varied greatly, and there was an obvious need to help all adults in the deaf child's environment to become better communicators. In most cases this meant learning to sign better. We have established and maintained sign classes for teachers, houseparents, nurses, and even housekeepers. Those classes, of course, are offered in addition to the parent communication classes scattered across the state. The School has employed a full-time communication coordinator to administer these programs. Because we believe strongly in the oral-aural aspects of Total Communication, we have stressed also the development of the use of speech and residual hearing, as a part of the Total Communication program. Two speech pathologists have been added to our staff to provide specific and more intensive training in speech development and auditory training. With the opening of the new Academic Building this fall, every classroom will be equipped with a top quality amplification system. Even though most of the students in the Maryland School for the Deaf have hearing losses in the severe to profound category, 80 percent of them are fitted with individual amplification as we push ahead with Total Communication. Although individual and group amplification has been stressed at the Maryland School for the Deaf for many years, continuous effort is made to interpret and implement this aspect of Total Communication. In-service training in the use and care of hearing aids and group amplification systems is a critical part of our program for teachers, houseparents, and parents.

As the parents of our children learn to sign, they come to us with many interesting and exciting new stories. We frequently hear from these parents statements such as: "We have seen such a change in Jimmy" or "Things are better at home now" or "I had no idea my child knew those things" or "Johnny has joined the family." These are beautiful things to hear and it is a fulfilling experience to see the obvious pleasure on a parent's face when such statements are being made. But the whole philosophy of Total Communication is capsulized in this recurring statement made by young deaf children whose parents have learned to sign: "Mother and father are deaf now."

REFERENCES

1. Denton, D.M. "To the Profession." **Proceedings of the Teacher Institute.** Published by Maryland School for the Deaf, Washington, D.C. 1969, pages 2,3.

2. **Communication Symposium**, Maryland School for the Deaf, Frederick, Maryland, March 13, 1970.

3. Denton, D.M., "Educational Crises." Paper presented for the Tripod Conference, Memphis, Tennessee, April 1971. Reprinted in the **Maryland Bulletin**, Volume XCII, Number One, October, 1971.

4. Denton, M.D., "The Spiritual Dimension." Paper presented at the Biennial Meeting of the Progessional Rehabilitation Workers With the Adult Deaf, Inc., Washington, D.C., April 10, 1972. Printed in the **Maryland Bulletin,** XCII, Number Six, April, 1972.

5. Denton, M.D., "Current Circumstances in Rehabilitation of the Deaf." Paper presented at the Conference of State Directors of Vocational Rehabilitation, Little Rock, Arkansas, February, 1972.

6. Kent, Margaret S., "Are Signs Legitimate?" **American Annals of the Deaf,** September, 1970, pages 497-8.

7. Kent, Margaret, S., "Language Growth and Development of the Deaf Child. " Paper presented at the In-Service Workshop, Carver School for the Deaf, Annapolis, Maryland, March 19, 1971.

8. Kent, Margaret S., "Total Communication at Maryland School for the Deaf." **The Deaf American,** Volume 23, Number Five, January, 1971.

9. **Proceedings of the Teacher Institute.** Maryland School for the Deaf, October, 1969.

SIGN LANGUAGE MADE SIMPLE

KEY TO INSTRUCTION SYMBOLS

If you have a question regarding the diagrams or the symbols used throughout, the instructions below will more than likely answer it for you.

1. Fingerspelled words usually have no sign; however, words such as "do," "did," "it," etc., can be spelled almost as easily as signing them since they are short.

2. The article "the" and the "to" of infinitives are not signed unless for emphasis or in educational settings. Therefore, they are marked with an asterisk(*)and "optional."

3. Letters in quotation marks signify hand configurations; for example, "A," "T," "F,"etc. Right "R"--right

4. Symbols ABOVE a word give the direction in which the sign moves and the hand used as well as whether right hand in left, R-in-L, etc.

5. Words printed in blue and the small print words in blue below are synonyms which use the same sign for communication. Here is an example

working
labor
job

6. Explanations in small print below a word are memory aids or clues for remembering the sign; for example, "Light goes on" is used for the word "understand."

understand
light goes on

F→R	Front of body to right
F→L	Front of body to left
CW	Clockwise (to the person signing)
C-C-W	Counterclockwise (to the person signing)
R-O-L	Right hand over left
R-in-L	Right hand in left
L-in-R	Left hand in right
R-on-L	Right hand on left
L-on-R	Left hand on right
IN	In towards the body
OUT	Away from the body
L→B	From left towards body
R→B	From right towards body
R→L	Right hand to left
R-U-L	Right hand under left
→R	To right
→L	To left
RL	Right hand aross left
LR	Left hand across right
2X	Repeat the action twice
3X	Repeat the action three times
WA	Wrist action
EA	Action from the elbow
BHA	Both hands do the action
RHA	Right hand action ONLY
LHA	Left hand action ONLY
AA	Alternating action
WF	Wiggle fingers

HINTS FOR LEARNING SIGNS

1. Basically signs are made comfortably. Exaggerated signs are ugly.

2. Fingerspelling is NOT "writing in the air." The hand should be comfortably held to the lower right of the mouth so that both the lips and hand can be clearly seen.

3. Some signs come from the wrist, others from the elbow, others from the shoulder.

4. Signs dealing with concepts that center on the mind or head are all signed from that area of the body, Emotions come from the heart; therefore, come from that part of the body.

5. Objective signs: you, me, they, them, etc. are all signed with the index finger.

6. Possessives such as yours, mine, his, theirs, etc. are all signed with open palm.

BASIC RULES FOR SIGNING

1. Signs are made left to right when both hands do equal action.

2. When the actions done are with one hand, it is the right hand that does the action.

3. The right hand is the "meaning" hand or prominent hand in performing the action.

Some left-handed persons prefer to learn signs as a right-handed person. If not, the left-handed person may do the opposite of the right-handed person.

Manual Alphabet

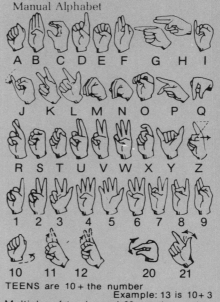

TEENS are 10 + the number
Example: 13 is 10 + 3
Multiples of ten beyond 20 are the number plus the letter "O" Example: 30 is 3 + "O"
Hundreds are the number + C.
Example: 200 is 2 + C
Thousands are the number + M in the left palm
Example: 5,000 is 5 + M in palm

2X

1. **Hello!**
like salute

Good-bye!

BHA

2. **How   are   you   ?**

3. **I   am   fine!**

4. **Thank   you.**

5. **You   are**

R→B

welcome.

R-in-L
2X

6. **Excuse   me.**

R

7. **I   am   sorry.**

R

8. **Please.**

enjoy
privilege
appreciate

9. **Are   you   deaf   ?**
ear + closed

10. **Are   you**

2X

hearing   ?
speaking

11. **What   time   is   it   ?**

CW

CW

12. **Today** **is** **Monday.**
now + day

13. **Tomorrow** **is** **Tuesday.**

ÇW

CW

CW

14. **Yesterday** **was** **Wednesday;** **Thursday;** **Friday;**

CW

IN
BHA
AA

Saturday; **Sunday.** 15. **Come** **with** **me.** 16. **It**

BHA

is **my** **book.** 17. **It** **is** **mine.** 18. **I**
mine my

OUT
BHA
AA

R-on-L
2X

will **go** **myself.** 19. **Practice** **it** **with** **me.**
train

OUT
BHA
AA

20. **He   (She)   will   go.**

WORD	SYNONYM	MEMORY AID	SENTENCE
am	—	—	3,7
are	—	—	2,5,9,10
book	—	—	16
come	—	—	15
deaf	—	ear + closed	9
excuse	—	—	6
fine	—	—	3
Friday	—	—	14
go	—	—	18,20
good-bye	—	—	1
hearing	speaking	—	10
hello	—	—	1
how	—	—	2
I	—	—	3,7,18
is	—	—	11,12,13,16,17
it	—	—	11,16,17,19
me	—	—	6,15,19
mine	—	—	17
Monday	—	—	12
my	—	—	16

WORD	SYNONYM	MEMORY AID	SENTENCE
myself	—	—	18
please	enjoy, like privilege	—	8
practice	train	—	19
Saturday	—	—	14
sorry	—	—	7
Sunday	—	—	14
thank	—	—	4
Thursday	—	—	14
time	—	—	11
today	—	now + day	12
tomorrow	—	—	13
Tuesday	—	—	13
was	—	—	14
Wednesday	—	—	14
welcome	—	—	5
what	—	—	11
will	—	—	18,20
with	—	—	15,19
yesterday	—	—	14
you	—	—	2,4,5,9,10

Word Drills

Lesson 1 (''at'' words)

bat, cat, date, fat, fate, fatal, gate, ate, eat, hat, hate, late, Kate, mat, mate, cat, goat, pat, rate, rat, tat, vat, sat, sate, grate, crate, plate, state, slate, skate.

1   2   3   4   5   6   7   8   9   10

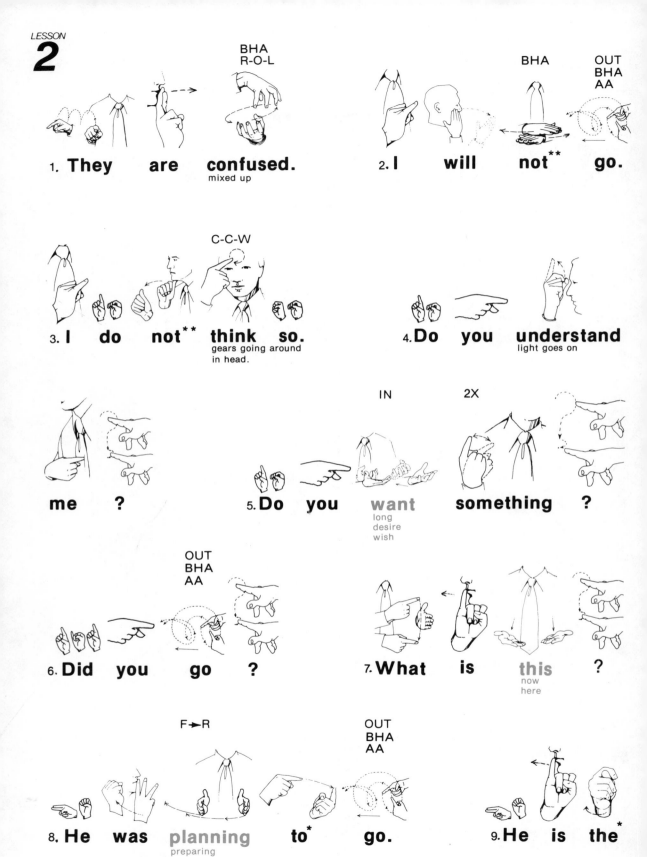

BHA
R-O-L

1. **They   are   confused.**
mixed up

BHA   OUT
BHA
AA

2. **I   will   not**   go.**

C-C-W

3. **I   do   not**   think   so.**
gears going around
in head.

4. **Do   you   understand**
light goes on

me   ?

IN   2X

5. **Do   you   want   something   ?**
long
desire
wish

OUT
BHA
AA

6. **Did   you   go   ?**

7. **What   is   this   ?**
now
here

F►R

OUT
BHA
AA

8. **He   was   planning   to*   go.**
preparing

9. **He   is   the***

★★''Not'' may be signed either way.
★ OPTIONAL

past   **president.**

R-in-L   WA

10. **That**   **happened**   **long**   **ago.**
past

11. **Do**   **it**   **now.**
here
this

BHA
AA   CW   WA

12 **Jesus**   **is**   **always**   **the***   **same.**
ever   alike

   WA   BHA   BHA

13. **They**   **look**   **alike**   **but**   **they**   **are**   **different!**
appear   same
seem

WA   2X   CW   OUT
                             BHA
                             AA

14. **The***   **story**   **is**   **about**   **John.**

15. **He**   **went**   **to**
go

R-on-L

church.   16. **She**   **has**   **a**   **call**   **from**   **God.**
possessive

* OPTIONAL

IN   WA

17.**You   are   wanted   on** * **the** * **telephone.**   18.**She**

BHA   RHA

called   him   "Jack".   19. **Introduce   us!**   20.**He**
named

is   dumb.
stupid

WORD	SYNONYM	MEMORY AID	SENTENCE	WORD	SYNONYM	MEMORY AID	SENTENCE
a	—	—	16	dumb	stupid	—	20
about	—	—	14	from	—	—	16
ago	past	—	10	God	—	—	16
alike	same	—	13	happened	—	—	10
always	—	—	12	has	—	possessive	16
but	—	—	13	introduce	—	—	19
call	—	—	16	Jesus	—	—	12
called	named	—	18	long	—	—	10
church	—	—	15	look	appear, seem	—	13
confused	mixed-up	—	1	not	—	—	2,3
different	—	—	13	now	here, this	—	11
do	—	—	3,4,5,11	on	—	—	17

*OPTIONAL

WORD	SYNONYM	MEMORY AID	SENTENCE	WORD	SYNONYM	MEMORY AID	SENTENCE
past	—	—	9	think	—	gears going around in head	3
planning	—	—	8	this	now + here	—	7
president	—	—	9	to	—	—	15
same	—	—	12	understand	—	light goes on	4
something	—	—	5	us	—	—	19
story	—	—	14	want	long, desire, wish	—	5,17
telephone	—	—	17	went	go	—	15
that	—	—	10				
the	—	—	9,12,14,17				
they	—	—	1,13				

Word Drills

Lesson 2 ("am" words)

bam, cam, dam, ream, fame, game, ham, jam, lam, lame, mama, exam, loam, foam, roam, ram, sam, same, tam, tame, vamp.

11   12   13   14   15   16   17   18   19

F→R
W F

1. **How do you spell that word ?**

2. **Do you**

BHA AA   BHA WA

OUT BHA AA

like
prefer

sign language ?

3. **Do you go to**

WA

R-on-L

OUT BHA AA

the* Assemblies of God church ?

4. **No, I go**

WA

R-on-L

BHA   RHA

to the* Baptist church.

5. **I don't understand;**

C-C-W

I thought you were Catholic.

6. **He said, "I**

* OPTIONAL

EA

BHA
AA

WA

need
must
have to
ought
should

to* **talk** **to** **her''!**

7. **I** **called** **for**

L-in-R
2.

↑1.

help.

8. **You**

must
ought
have to
should

phone
call

me.

BHA

9. **Where** **did**

R-in-L

BHA
2X

R-in-L

you **get** **that** **animal** **?**

10. **That** **is** **my**

R-on-L

EA

R-on-L

R-in-L

RHA

work.
labor
job

11. **You**

must
have to
ought
should

keep **that** **dog**
snap
fingers

at **home.**

OUT
BHA
AA

BHA

RHA
2X

12. **You**

should
duty

go **to** **class.**

13. **His** **experience**

LESSON 3

R-in-L

BHA
2X

R-O-L

BHA

in **football** **is** **limited.**

14. **He** **is** **very**

R-on-L
2X

1.
2.

experienced **in** **his** **job.**
work
labor

15. **It** **is** **a**

R-on-L

BHA

nice **day.**

16. **I** **will** **meet** **you** **at**

R-in-L   CW   2X

noon.

17. **Tell** **me** **again** **about** **your** **cat.**
say   whiskers
speak

2X
R-on-L   R-on-L   R-on-L   EA   WA

18. **He** **works** **slowly.**

19. **Practice** **is** **necessary** **for**
training   need
must
should
ought

34

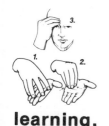

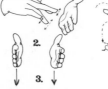

learning.
Take from book
put in head

20. **Are you a student ?**
study + person ending

WORD	SYNONYM	MEMORY AID	SENTENCE	WORD	SYNONYM	MEMORY AID	SENTENCE
again	—	—	17	limited	—	—	13
animal	—	—	9	meet	—	—	16
Assemblies of God	—	—	3	must	have to, ought should	—	8,11
at	—	—	11,16	necessary	need, must, should	—	19
Baptist	—	—	4				
cat	—	whiskers	17	need	must, have to, ought, should	—	6
Catholic	—	—	5				
class	—	—	12	nice	—	—	15
day	—	—	15	no	—	—	4
dog	—	—	11	noon	—	—	16
don't	—	—	5	phone	—	—	8
experience	—	—	13,14	said	—	—	6
football	—	—	13	should	duty	—	12
for	—	—	7,19	sign	—	—	2
get	—	—	9	slowly	—	—	18
he	—	—	6,14	spell	—	—	1
help	—	—	7	student	—	study + person	20
his	—	—	13,14				
home	—	—	11	talk	—	—	6
in	—	—	13,14	tell	say, speak	—	17
job	work, labor	—	14	thought	—	—	5
keep	—	—	11	very	—	—	14
language	—	—	2	were	—	—	5
learning	—	take from book, put in head	19	where	—	—	9
				word	—	—	1
				work	labor, job	—	10,18
like	prefer	—	2	your	—	—	17

Word Drills

Lesson 3 ("th" words)

that, the, this, there, they, then, them, those, throw, throne, thrice, thrown, Thursday, think, thank, than, thaw, three, their, threw, thick, thin, thief, thigh, thrift, thirst, thong, thorn, thing, thread, threat, three, thresh, thirst, throb, throng, thumb, thwart, thyme, thus, with, Ruth, Thomas, Timothy, Nathanael, Abiathar, Dathan, Matthew, Goliath, Elizabeth, Jethro, Esther.

21 22 23 24 25 26 27 28 29 30

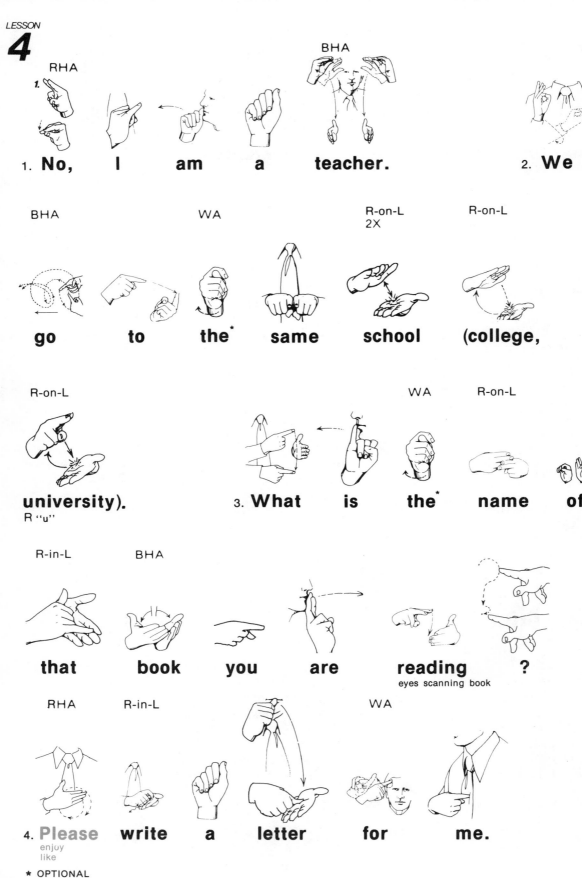

RHA
1.

BHA

1. **No,** **I** **am** **a** **teacher.**

2. **We**

BHA

WA

R-on-L
2X

R-on-L

go **to** **the*** **same** **school** **(college,**

R-on-L

WA

R-on-L

university).
R "u"

3. **What** **is** **the*** **name** **of**

R-in-L

BHA

that **book** **you** **are** **reading** **?**
eyes scanning book

RHA

R-in-L

WA

4. **Please** **write** **a** **letter** **for** **me.**
enjoy
like

★ OPTIONAL

36

WA

R-in-L

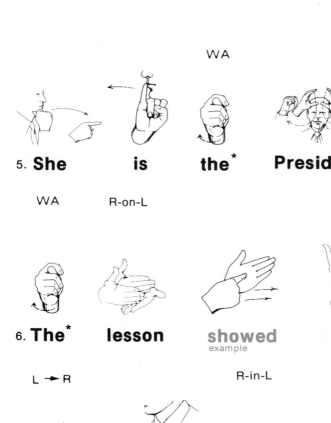

5. **She**   **is**   **the** *   **President's**   **secretary.**

WA   R-on-L   F ➤ R

6. **The** *   **lesson**   **showed**   **good**   **planning.**

example

L ➤ R   R-in-L   R-on-L

                                2X

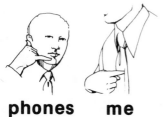

7. **Bring**   **me**   **some**   **paper.**   8. **He**

                     part

R-in-L   CW   BHA

2X   AA

phones   **me**   **often**   **about**   **his**   **troubles.**

            again, again   trials,

                                                      cares

                                  WA   L-in-R

                                                                    2.

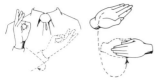   

9. **We**   **all**   **thank**   **you**   **for**   **your**   **help.**

* OPTIONAL

L-on-R

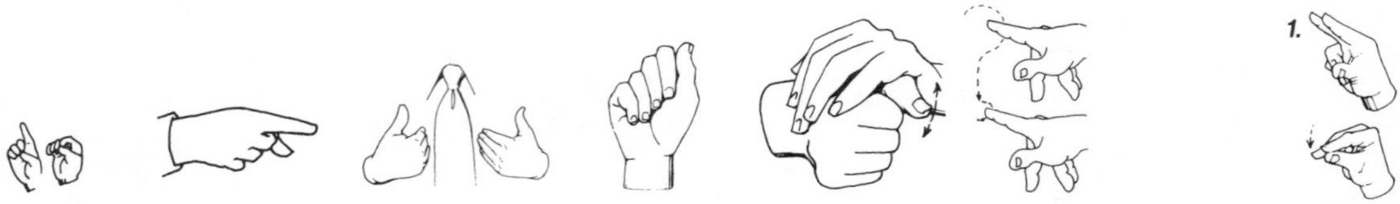

10. **Do**   **you**   **have**
possessive
   a   **turtle**   **?**   11. **No**

RHA

but   **I**   **do**   **have**
possessive
   a   **frog.**

2X   ➤ R

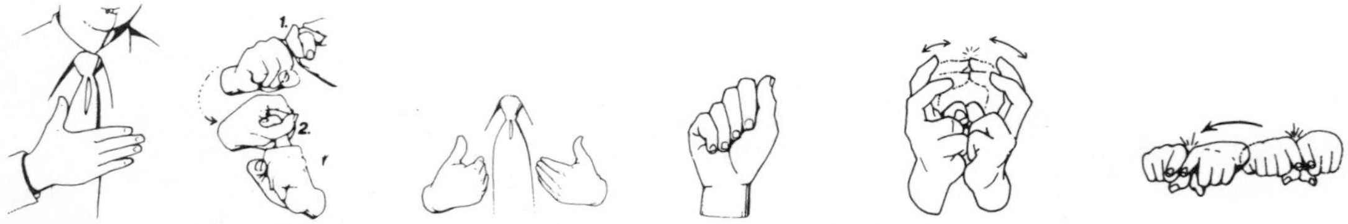

12. **My**   **friend**   **has**   **a**   **squirrel**   **too.**
also

WA   R-on-L   EA   C-C-W

13. **The***   **church**   **needs**
must,
should,
ought to,
have to
   men   **who**   **are**

R-in-L   AA
BHA   R-in-L

true   **servants.**   14. **That**   **boy**   **is**

★ OPTIONAL

his son.

15. **The*** girl walking with

WA

BHA AA

him is six years old.
chin whiskers

BHA AA

16. **Which** person do you like best ?
Which one   "P"s   prefer

L ► B

17. **When** did he leave ?

C-C-W

BHA IN AA

18. **They** live together.

19. **People**
"P's"

★ OPTIONAL

came	**from**	**far**	**and**	**near**	**to**[*]

hear	**him.**	20. **Did**	**you**	**remember**

→ R

to[*]	**bring**	**your**	**Bible** Jesus book	**?**

WORD	SYNONYM	MEMORY AID	SENTENCE		WORD	SYNONYM	MEMORY AID	SENTENCE
all	—	—	9		him	—	—	15, 19
best	—	—	16		leave	—	—	17
Bible	—	Jesus book	20		lesson	—	—	6
boy	—	—	14		letter	—	—	4
bring	—	—	7, 20		live	—	—	18
came	—	—	19		men	—	—	13
college	—	—	2		name	—	—	3
far	—	—	19		near	—	—	19
friend	—	—	12		often	—	again, again	8
frog	—	—	11		old	—	chin whiskers	15
girl	—	—	15		paper	—	—	7
good	—	—	6		people	—	—	16
have	—	possessive	10,11		reading	—	eyes scanning book	3
hear	—	—	19					

[*] OPTIONAL

remember	—	—	20	too	also	—	12
school	—	—	2	troubles	trials, cares	—	8
secretary	—	—	5	true	—	—	13
servants	—	—	13	turtle	—	—	10
she	—	—	5	university	—	"U"	2
showed	example	—	6	walking	—	—	15
six	—	—	15	we	—	—	2
some	part	—	7	when	—	—	17
son	—	—	14	which	which one	—	16
squirrel	—	—	12	who	—	—	13
teacher	—	—	1	write	—	—	4
together	—	—	18	years	—	—	15

Word Drills

Lesson 4 ("oa" words)

boat, coat, road, goat, load, goad, float, throat, Noah, loam, foal, toad, loamy, moat, gloat, goal, roan, soak, loan.

31 32 33 34 35 36 37 38 39 40

LESSON
5

BHA · R-on-L

1. **Why didn't you call me ?**

F→B · OUT BHA AA

2. **Most of us wanted to* go.**
more + superlative

CW · OUT BHA AA · →R

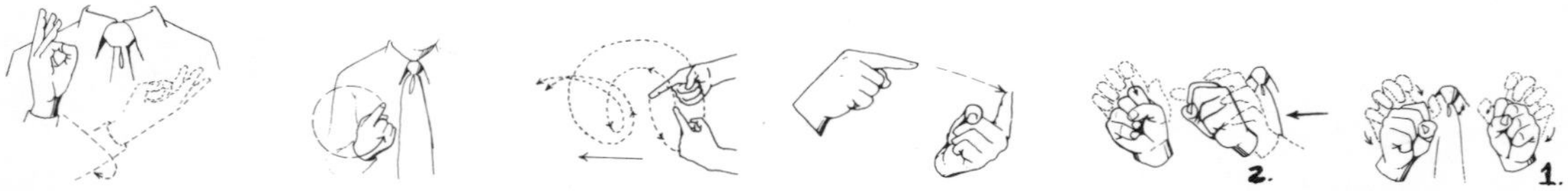

3. **We always go to* Sunday School.**

CW · R-on-L

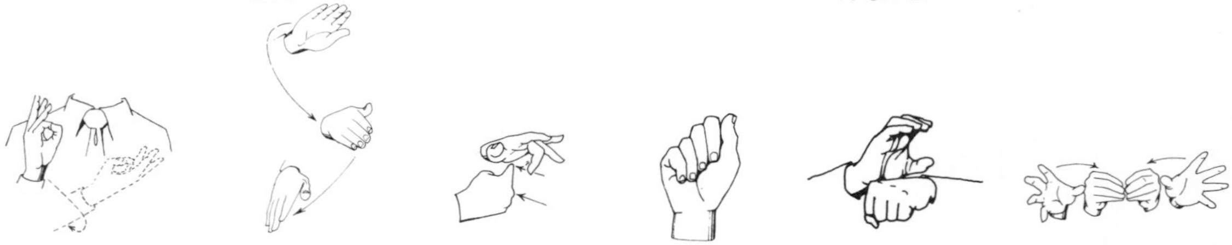

4. **We never miss a church service.**
miss: absent

RHA · R-in-L

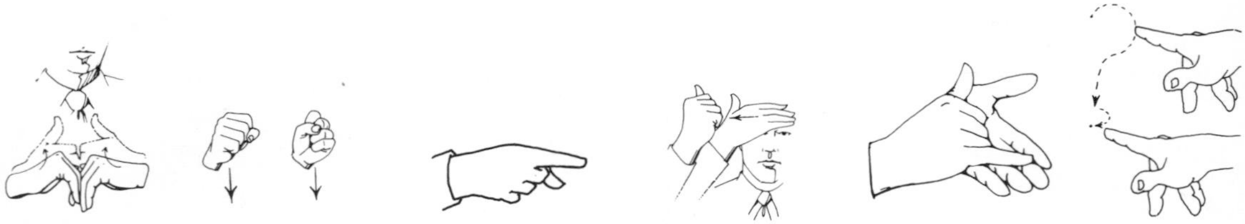

5. **How could you forget that ?**
could: can, able, power
forget: wipe from mind

6. **Did** **you** **know** **he** **is** **a** **Jew**
goatee

2X

?

C-C-W   R ► B   R-on-L
WF

7. **I** **thought** **he** **came** **from** **Germany** .

R-U-L   R

8. **He** **is** **running** **fast.**   9. **Do**

R-in-L
2X

you **have** **any** **money** **?**   10. **Did**
possessive

R-in-L   EA   WA
BHA   BHA

you **buy** **your** **sign** **language** **book** **?**
money paid out

R-in-L

11. **I** **told** **you** **not** **to*** **buy** **both**
say,   money paid out   couple
tell

books! 12. **How** **old** **are** **you** **?**
Y-past

13. **Yesterday** **was** **Sunday!** 14. **He** **is**
Y-past

R-in-L

a **bad** **boy.** 15. **She** **quit**
F▸R

R-in-L

her **job** **as** **a** **secretary.**
work,
labor

* OPTIONAL

44

2X

16. **She** **is** **happy** **to** **be** **home.**
glad
rejoice
eat, sleep

R-in-L   R-on-L

17. **The*** **news** **made** **me** **sad.**
long face

WA   BHA
AA
OUT

18. **Let's** **go** **out!**   19. **He**

R-in-L   BHA

arrived **late** **for** **class.**   20. **He**
not yet   "C" group

L➤B   BHA   R-on-L

left **class** **early.**

* OPTIONAL

WORD	SYNONYM	MEMORY AID	SENTENCE	WORD	SYNONYM	MEMORY AID	SENTENCE
any	—	—	9	left	—	—	20
arrived	—	—	19	let's	—	—	18
as	—	—	15	made	—	—	17
bad	—	—	14	miss	absent	—	4
both	couple	—	11	money	—	—	9
buy	—	paid out, money	11	most	—	more + superlative	2
could	can, able power	—	5	never	—	—	4
early	—	—	20	news	—	—	17
fast	—	—	8	not yet	—	—	19
forget	—	wipe from mind	5	out	—	—	18
Germany	—	—	7	quit	—	—	15
happy	glad, rejoice	—	16	running	—	—	8
her	—	—	15	sad	—	long face	17
Jew	—	goatee	6	service	—	—	4
know	—	—	6	Sunday School	—	—	3
late	not yet	—	19	told	say, tell	—	11
				why	—	—	1

Word Drills

Lesson 5 ("ea" words)

beat, cease, grease, gear, heat, heal, jeans, yearn, beam, meal,
hear, heap, leap, mean, meant, peal, near, zeal, lean, weak,
deal, seam, pea, ream, lead, reap, dream, steam, seal, seat,
real, scream, team, Hosea, dead, eat, feat, veal, Gibea, tease,
gleam, steam.

41 42 43 44 45 46 47 48 49 50

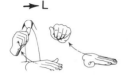

1. **Leave**   **the***   **book**   **on**   **the***   **table.**

4 legs and a top

CW

2. **Did**   **you**   **hear**   **the***   **story**   **about**   **the***

 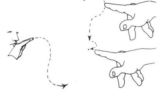

fox   **and**   **the***   **elephant**   **?**   3. **Would**

trunk of elephant   "Wd"

you   **please**   **finish**   **that**   **job**   **?**

     like   complete   work,

     enjoy   labor

R-in-L

4. **I**   **already**   **did**   **that!**   5. **Flowers**

    finish

*** OPTIONAL**

WA

bloom   **in**   **the***   **spring.**
grow

6. **Did**   **you**

R-on-L   L►R   WF

have   **a**   **nice**   **summer**   **vacation**   **?**
possessive

R-on-L   R-on-L   WA   2X
2X

7. **School**   **(College)**   **begins**   **in**   **the***   **fall.**
leaves

8. **Winters**   **in**   **Missouri**   **are**   **much**   **warmer**
cold   Mo.   amount
                                               comparative
                                               or quantity

R-on-L

than   **in**   **the***   **north**   **(east,**   **west,**   **south).**
same as compass points

WA   L►R

9. **They**   **were**   **married**   **during**   **the***   **summer.**

                                while

10. **I**   **have**   **one**   **son**   **and**   **one**   **daughter.**
       possessive   man + baby   woman + baby

11. **I**   **have**   **three**   **brothers**   **and**   **one**   **sister.**
       possessive   man + same   woman + same

12. **They**   **are**   **now**   **husband**   **and**   **wife.**
                       this   man + married   woman + married

BHA   R
AA   2X

13. **He**   **is**   **a**   **Methodist**   **preacher.**

* OPTIONAL

R-on-L   R-in-L

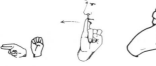

14. **He** **is** **saving** **his** **money** **for** **a**

R   C-C-W   F➤R

trip **to** **Europe.** 15. **He** **plans**

OUT   R-on-L   R-on-L

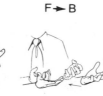

to* **visit** **England,** **Ireland,** **Holland,** **and**
English   potato   "Y" like pipe

F➤B

Italy. 16. **I** **want** **to*** **have**
"I" like Catholic   possessive

turkey, **chicken,** **or** **duck** **for** **Thanksgiving**
bird

*OPTIONAL

50

dinner.
eat noon

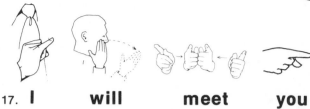

17. **I** **will** **meet** **you**

at **dinner.**

18. **I** **know** **it** **is**

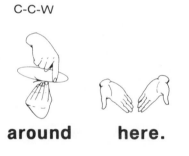

around **here.**

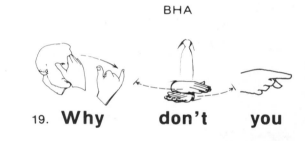

19. **Why** **don't** **you**

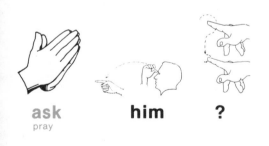

ask **him** **?**
pray

20. **Please** **put**

away **your** **books.**

WORD	SYNONYM	MEMORY AID	SENTENCE	WORD	SYNONYM	MEMORY AID	SENTENCE
already	finish	—	4	married	—	—	9
around	—	—	18	Methodist	—	—	13
ask	pray	—	19	Missouri	Mo.	—	8
away	—	—	20	much	amount, i.e.	comparative or quantity	8
begins	—	—	7				
bloom	—	—	5				
brothers	—	man + same	11	north	—	—	8
chicken	bird	—	16	preacher	—	—	13
daughter	—	woman + baby	10	put	—	—	20
				saving	—	—	14
dinner	—	—	16,17	sister	—	woman - same	11
duck	—	—	16				
during	while	—	9	south	—	—	8
east	—	—	8	spring	—	—	5
elephant	—	trunk of elephant	2	summer	—	—	6, 9
				table	—	4 legs and a top	1
England	English	—	15				
Europe	—	—	14	than	—	—	8
fall (season)	leaves	—	7	Thanksgiving	—	—	16
finish	already, complete	—	3	trip	—	—	14
				turkey	—	—	16
flowers	—	—	5	vacation	—	—	6
fox	—	—	2	visit	—	—	15
here	—	—	18	warmer	—	—	8
Holland	—	"Y" like pipe	15	west	—	—	8
husband	—	man + married	12	wife	—	woman + married	12
Ireland	potato	—	15	winters	cold	—	8
Italy	—	"I" like Catholic	15	would	—	—	3

Word Drills

Lesson 6 ("an" words)

any, ant, ban, can, Dan, Jan, fan, man, pan, ran, tan, van, hand, Jane, land, many, loan, pant, rant, sand, sank, want, Anna, Danny, Annas, gander, handle, kantor, landed, tanned, wander, Andrew, Daniel, Antipas, Andronicus.

51   52   53   54   55   56   57   58   59   60

1.

| What | did | you | have | to* | eat | ? |

C-C-W
R-on-L

2.

We   **had**   **an**   **orange,**   **coffee,**   **toast,**

R-on-L   R   2X   fork in slice
of bread

and   **eggs**   **for**   **breakfast.**   **3. For**

        break eggs   eat + morning
        on bowl

2X   R-on-L   W A
                                       R

lunch   **we**   **had**   **potatoes,**   **onions,**

dinner,   Ireland
eat
noon

                             2X

tomatoes,   **meat,**   **and**   **ice cream.**

                                eating cone

4. **Do** **you** **like** **gravy**
oil
on **your**
possessive
potatoes
Ireland

R   R-on-L   R-on-L

?

R   2X   R-on-L 2X

5. **I** **like** **crackers,** **cheese,**

R-in-L WA   R

and **tea.**

6. **He** **is** **feeling**

R-on-L

much **better** **today.** 7. **That**
amount   rather   now + day

is **a** **large** **book** **you** **are**

L → R

carrying.

8. **Do** **you** **think** **you**

C-C-W

can
able
could

swallow **it** **?**

9. **Yesterday**

R-U-L   C-C-W

Mary **ran** **around** **the*** **table.**
4 least top

10. **Would**
"WD"

you **ask**
pray

John **to*** **meet**

R-on-L   WA

me **at** **the*** **corner** **?**

11. **What**

* OPTIONAL

55

R   2X

did   **you**   **eat**   **for**   **breakfast**   **?**

eat + morning

     2X   R

12. **I**   **didn't**   **eat**   **anything**   **but**   **I**

did not

WA   R-in-L   C-C-W

drank   **some**   **coffee.**   13. **My**   **father**

drink   part

BHA
OUT   ➝ R
AA

and   **mother**   **are**   **going**   **away.**

BHA
IN
EA

14. **You**   **sign**   **better**   **now**   **than**   **you**

rather

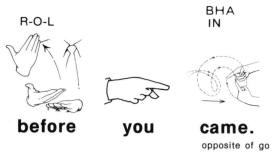

R-O-L

BHA
IN

did **before** **you** **came.**

opposite of go

15. **He**

is **my** **best** **friend.**

hooked torefingers

16. **You**

BHA
IN
EA

R-in-L

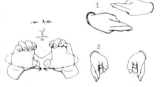 

should **sign** **large** **when** **in** **a**

need,
must,
have to,
ought to

classroom. 17. **She** **saw** **a**

"C" + "R"

R-on-L

deer **on** **the*** **way** **home** **from**

antlers eat, sleep

* OPTIONAL

BHA
AA

ice skating.

R-on-L

18. **Will** you **keep**
"V"

WA

your **cat** **at** **home** **?**
whiskers eat, sleep

2X
R-in-L

19. **Can**
able,
could,
power

OUT

you **loan** **me** **some** **money** **?**
"V" out part

WA

2X
R-in-L

20. **My** **father** **borrowed** **all** **the** * **money**
"V" in

he **needed** **to** * **buy** **a** **house.**
must,
should,
have to,
ought to

* OPTIONAL

WORD	SYNONYM	MEMORY AID	SENTENCE	WORD	SYNONYM	MEMORY AID	SENTENCE
anything	—	—	12	gravy	oil	—	4
before (point in time)	—	—	14	had	—	—	2
				house	—	—	20
better	—	—	6, 14	ice cream	—	eating cone	3
borrowed	—	"V" in	20	large	great, big	—	7
breakfast	—	eat + morning	2, 11	loan	—	"V out	19
				lunch	dinner	—	3
can	could, able, power	—	19	meat	—	—	3
				mother	—	—	13
carrying	—	—	7	onions	—	—	3
cheese	—	—	5	orange	—	—	2
classroom	—	"C" "R"	16	potatoes	—	—	3, 4
coffee	—	—	2, 12	saw	see	—	17
corner	—	—	10	swallow	—	—	8
crackers	—	—	5	tea	—	—	5
deer	—	antlers	17	toast	—	fork in slice of bread	2
drank	drink	—	12				
eat	—	—	1, 11, 12	tomatoes	—	—	3
eggs	—	break eggs on bowl	2				
father	—	—	13, 20				
feeling	—	—	6				

Word Drills

Lesson 7 ("is" words)

gist, hiss, list, miss, Lois, rise, mist, heist, anise, quist, Louis, vista, cissna, sister, biscuit, Priscilla.

61 62 63 64 65 66 67 68 69 70

WA

1. **The** ** **law** **says** **he** **must** **pay**

says
tell,
speak

must
need,
should,
have to

WA

eight **percent** **interest.** 2. **My** **Aunt**

Aunt
''A'' female

WA

R-on-L
2X

and **Uncle** **have** **saved** **enough**

Uncle
''U'' male

saved
store
reserve

enough
sufficient

2X

WF

money **for** **their** **vacation.** 3. **My**

WA

cousin **lives** **in** **Michigan.**

cousin
''C''

Michigan.
Abbreviate, Mich.

* OPTIONAL

60

WA
 WA

4. **I** **have** **twelve** **nieces** **and** **nephews.**
possessive   "N" female   "N" male

5. **Both** **my** **grandmother** **and** **grandfather** **are**
Couple

→ R
    R-on-L

dead. 6. **I** **enjoy** **a** **salad** **made**
turn over   like, pleasure

R-on-L
   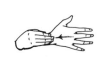

with **grapes,** **pears,** **and** **peaches.**
"peach fuzz" on face

WA
   BHA

7. **His** **nephew** **is** **a** **quaker.**
"N" male   twiddle thumbs

61

IN   WA

 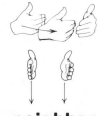

8. **He**   **came**   **here**   **from**   **France.**

       opposite of go   "F" ➤ R

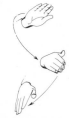   

9. **My**   **neighbor**   **is**   **a**   **close**   **friend**   **of**

      "near person"   near   hooked forefingers

R-on-L

  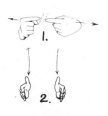 

mine.   10. **I**   **make**   **it**   **a**   **habit**

my   mind bound

➤ R

never   **to***   **have**   **any**   **enemies.**

                                  opposite person

11. **Yesterday**   **was**   **a**   **beautiful**   **day.**

                                  pretty,
                                  lovely

* OPTIONAL

C-C-W   WA   BHA

 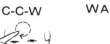

12. **I**   **think**   **the***   **picture**   **is**   **ugly.**

"C"

   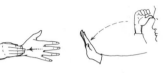

13. **He**   **is**   **a**   **real**   **gentleman**   **and**   **his**

"R"   man + ruffles

R

wife   **a**   **fine**   **lady.**   14. **Their**

woman +   "5"   woman + ruffles
married

IN   2X

parents   **came**   **from**   **Canada.**   15. **They**

"P" chin, forehead   opposite of go   lapel

BHA   BHA
IN

both   **come**   **from**   **good**   **families.**

couple   opposite of go   "F" class

* OPTIONAL

16. **I**   **understand**
recognize
light goes on
that   **she**   **was**   **their**

C-C-W
EA

RL

only   **child.**
heads of children

17. **They**   **stayed**
continued
after

WA   WF   WA

the   **bell**   **rang.**   18. **Most**   **of**   **the**

BHA
EA   L→B   F→R   F→R

people   **left**   **as**   **soon**   **as**   **the**
"P's"

meeting   **was**   **over.**
service
gathering
finished
19. **Be**   **sure**

L-on-R			C-C-W	R-on-L	

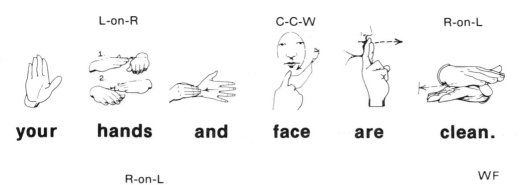

your	**hands**	**and**	**face**	**are**	**clean.**

R-on-L				WF	

20. **Last**
Past

	week	**your**	**feet**	**were**	**dirty.**

WORD	SYNONYM	MEMORY AID	SENTENCE	WORD	SYNONYM	MEMORY AID	SENTENCE
after	—	—	17	law	—	—	1
aunt	—	"A" female	2	meeting	service, gathering	—	18
beautiful	pretty, lovely	—	11	neighbor	—	"near person"	9
bell	—	—	17				
Canada	—	lapel	14	nephews	—	"N" male	4
child	—	heads of children	16	nieces	—	"N" female	4
clean	—	—	19	only	—	—	16
close	near	—	9	over	finished	—	18
cousin	—	"C"	3	parents	—	"P" chin, forehead	14
dead	—	turn over	5	pay	—	—	1
dirty	—	—	20	peaches	—	"peach fuzz" on face	6
enemies	—	opposite person	10				
enough	—	—	2	pears	—	—	6
face	—	—	19	percent	—	—	1
families	—	"F" + class	15	picture	—	"C"	12
feet	—	—	20	Quaker	—	twiddle thumbs	7
France	—	F→R	8				
gentleman	—	man + ruffles	13	rang	—	—	17
grandfather	—	—	5	real	—	—	13
grandmother	—	—	5	soon	—	—	18
grapes	—	—	6	stayed	continued	—	17
habit	—	mind bound	10	sure	—	—	19
hands	—	—	19	their	—	—	2
interest	—	—	1	ugly	—	—	12
lady	—	woman + ruffles	13	uncle	—	"U" male	2
last	past	—	20	week	—	—	20

Word Drills

Lesson 8 ("er" words)

aero, herd, mere, seer, very, veer, leer, deer, berry, Certs, eerie, Jerry, German, butler, period, career, lawyer,

71 72 73 74 75 76 77 78 79 80

WA

1. **Did**   **Tom**   **tell**   **you**   **I**   **found**   **a**

   say,
   speak

   discover

dollar   **yesterday**   **?**

WA   BHA

2. **The***   **movie**

2X

was   **funny!**

3. **Everyone**   **at**   **the***

BHA
AA

BHA

party   **said**   **it**   **was**   **fun!**

"P" play

R-on-L

IN

4. **Just**   **how**   **much**   **do**   **you**   **want**

   Right Correct

   amount

* OPTIONAL

R-on-L

for   **that**   **picture**   **?**   5. **The***

"C"

R-U-L

car   **was**   **hidden**   **behind**   **the***   **house.**

drive

L R

EA   BHA OUT AA

6. **You**   **ought**   **to**   **go**   **with**   **him.**

need, should, must

L►B   AA   F►B

7. **Let**   **them**   **leave**   **if**   **they**   **desire.**

allow   want, wish

R

8. **I**   **will**   **see**   **you**   **tomorrow.**

* OPTIONAL

WA

9. **Did** **you** **look at** **the*** **sunrise**

yesterday **?** 10. **I** **hope** **you**

expect
anticipate

will **watch** **for** **him.** 11. **Did**

look for

BHA
IN
AA

R►L

you **come** **here** **by** **airplane** **?**

opposite of go

12. **How** **many** **miles** **is** **it** **to**

* OPTIONAL

68

CW

Kansas **City** **?**
K.C.

WA

13. **The**[*] **children**
Pat heads of children

WA

play
"Y"

C-C-W

well

together.
with, circle C-C-W

14. **I**

R

don't **like** **that** **man!**

15. **The**[*]

L→B

minute **I** **left** **the**[*] **room** **he**

WA

began
start

BHA
AA

talking.

16. **The**[*] **hours**

* OPTIONAL

69

WA

seem like
appear,
look like

days

when

you

are

BHA
IN
AA

bored.
dry at chin

17. **They**

will

come

from

WA   C-C-W

R-on-L

the *

fields

afterwhile.
later

18. **Next**

R-on-L

week

is

the *

last
final

of

the *

month.

F→R

19. **Are**

you

planning

to *

come
opposite of go

back
again

* OPTIONAL

70

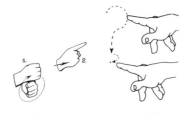

next   year   ?
year + 1 ➔ future

20. **Last   year**
Past

R-in-L

it   was   cold   at   this   time.
now   "T" circle

WORD	SYNONYM	MEMORY AID	SENTENCE	WORD	SYNONYM	MEMORY AID	SENTENCE
afterwhile	later	—	17	if	—	—	7
airplane	—	—	11	just	—	—	4
back	again	—	19	Kansas City	—	K.C.	12
began	—	—	15	man	—	—	14
behind	—	—	5	many	—	—	12
bored	—	dry at chin	16	minute	—	—	15
car	drive	—	5	month	—	—	18
children	—	—	13	movie	—	—	2
cold	—	—	20	next	—	—	18
desire	want, wish	—	7	next year	—	year + 1 future	19
dollar	—	—	1	party	—	"P" play	3
everyone	—	—	3	play	—	—	13
fields	—	—	17	room	—	—	15
found	discover	—	1	seem	—	—	16
fun	—	—	3	sunrise	—	—	9
funny	—	—	2	them	—	—	7
hidden, hide	—	—	5	watch for	look for	—	10
hope	expect, anticipate	—	10				
hours	—	—	16				

Word Drills

Lesson 9 ("oo" words)

boon, racoon, coon, food, noon, good, hood, look, too, took, mood, noodle, wool, pool, room, soon, stool, wooly, zoo, nook, book.

81   82   83   84   85   86   87   88   89   90

1.

A   year   ago   today   it   was   30

Year + one past   now - day

degrees.

2. **Two   years   from   now**

years + 2 + future

I   will   be   20   years   old.

beard

L ► B

3. **Last   night   I   saw   them   leave**

past

WA

together.   4. **Give   me   the***   **last**

with, circle C-C-W   final

* OPTIONAL

R
WA

apple.

5. **Did**   **you**   **shave**   **last**
"Y" down face   past

R

night   **?**

6. **When**   **did**   **you**

EA
R

R

take   **your**   **bath**   **(shower)**   **?**   7. **Did**
"A" on chest

L ↓ ↙ R

R-O-L

      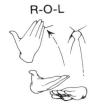   

you   **brush your teeth**   **before**   **breakfast**
eat, morning

R

?   8. **Your**   **hair**   **doesn't**   **look**
don't   appear, seem

R   R-in-L

as   **if**   **it**   **had**   **been**   **combed**   **in**

claw hand

R-in-L

months!   9. **Please**   **wear**   **your**   **new**

like,
enjoy,
pleasure

BHA

shoes,   **a**   **coat**   **and**   **a**   **tie.**

lapels   2 fingers

R-on-L

10. **You**   **are**   **just**   **a**   **young**   **man.**

right   youthful

WA   R-on-L   2X

11. **Give**   **me**   **the*****   **full**   **story.**

* OPTIONAL

WA   WA

12. **Can**   **you**   **fix**   **the**[*]   **hem**   **of**   **my**
able
could

shirt   **?**   13. **The**[*]   **room**   **was**

F→L   R-on-L

left   **empty.**   14. **Were**   **you**
naked

R-in-L

hurt   **in**   **the**[*]   **accident**   **?**
pain

15. **We**   **all**   **looked**   **at**   **him**   **when**
watched

[*] OPTIONAL

he

BHA
IN
AA

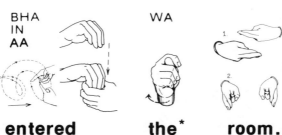

entered
came in

WA

the*

room.

16. **Please**
like,
enjoy,
pleasure

C-C-W
R-on-L

wash

BHA
OUT
AA

your

L-on-R
R-on-L
BHA

feet,

hands,

and

C-C-W

face

R-O-L

before

EA

going

to

bed.

17. **You**

should
need,
must,
ought to

be

kind

to

EA
BHA
IN

old
age

people.
"P"

R

18. **Some**
part

children
child

are

mean

to

* OPTIONAL

2X

animals.

19. **Do**   **you**

R

understand
recognize
light goes on

R-in-L

what   **I**   **mean**   **?**   20. **I**
              intend,
              purpose

2X

laughed   **until**   **I**   **cried.**
                                        weep
                                        tears flowing

WORD	SYNONYM	MEMORY AID	SENTENCE	WORD	SYNONYM	MEMORY AID	SENTENCE
accident	—	—	14	mean	cruel	—	18
apple	—	—	4	mean	intend, purpose	—	19
brush (teeth)	—	—	7	night	—	—	3, 5
coat	—	lapels	9	shave	—	"Y" down the face	5
combed	—	claw hand	8	shirt	—	—	12
cried	weep	tears flowing	20	shoes	—	—	9
empty	naked	—	13	shower	—	—	6
entered	—	came in	15	take	—	—	6
full	—	—	11	tie (neck)	—	two fingers	9
give	—	—	4, 11	until	—	—	20
hair	—	—	8	wash	—	—	16
hem	—	—	12	young	youthful	—	10
hurt	pain	—	14				
kind	—	—	17				
laugh	—	—	20				

Word Drills

Lesson 10 ("ei" words)

being, feint, deign, mein, receive, either, conceive, heist, ceiling, neither.

91   92   93   94   95   96   97   98   99   100

11

WA   2X   2X   BHA AA

1. **The***   **story**   **was**   **difficult**   **to***   **explain.**

problem   "F" describe

R

2. **Do**   **you**   **like**   **sugar**   **on**   **your**   **lemon**

prefer   sweet   lemonade

R-in-L

?   3. **He**   **was**   **Lutheran,**

"L"

WA   C-C-W   R

but   **now**   **belongs**   **to**   **the***   **Episcopal**

join,
organization,
relationship

R-on-L   WA

Church.   4. **Turn**   **off**   **the***   **light.**

bright,
clear

* OPTIONAL

BHA

5. **It**   **was**   **very**   **dark**   last   **night.**
                   ''V''   past

R-on-L

6. **I**   **live**   **in**   **Springfield,**   **Mo.**
   "G" = Greene County Seat

7. **What**   **is**   **your**   **home**   **address**   **?**
                   eat, sleep   ''A'' like ''live''

R

8. **How**   **long**   **have**   **you**   **lived**   **there**

R-on-L

?   9. **Time**   **is**   short.
            wrist watch   soon

AA

EA

BHA
IN
AA

R-in-L

10. **Maybe** **you** **should** **come** **back** **tomorrow.**
possibly
perhaps

need,
must,
ought to,
have to

opposite of go

again

WA

R-on-L

C-C-W
EA

R-in-L

11. **Moses** **struck** **the** * **rock** **only** **once.**

R-in-L
2X

OUT

12. **Sometimes** **we** **go** **to** **a**
once in a while

R

RL

R-on-L

restaurant **after** **church.**
"R" at mouth

13. **May**
let,
allow

CW

I **use** **your** **car** **tonight** **?**
"U"
drive
now + night

* OPTIONAL

WA

R-on-L

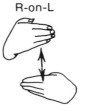

14. **Please**
like,
enjoy,
pleasure

open

the *

window.

15. **Close**
opposite of
open

the *

door

please.
like,
enjoy,
pleasure

16. **The** *

R→L

R-O-L

airplane

flew

over

my

house

recently.

L   R

R-on-L
L-on-R
AA

F→R

R-on-L

17. **Put**

your

hands

on

the *

table.

R-U-L → R

OUT
AA

18. **Will**

you

run

a

race
compete,
competition,
contest

with

* OPTIONAL

me

?

19. **I**

 would
"WD"

 rather
better

AA

walk
steps

than

R-U-L ➡ R

run.

20. **It**

 is

AA
2X

difficult
problems

R

for

me

to*

R-on-L

stand

R

for

a

long

time.
wrist watch

*OPTIONAL

WORD	SYNONYM	MEMORY AID	SENTENCE	WORD	SYNONYM	MEMORY AID	SENTENCE
address	—	"A" like "Live"	7	Moses	—	—	11
				once	—	—	11
belong	join, organization, relationship	—	3	open	—	—	14
				race	compete, competition	—	18
close (shut)	—	opposite of open	15	rather	better	—	19
				recently	—	—	16
dark	—	—	5	restaurant	—	"R" at mouth	12
difficult	problems	—	1, 20	short	soon	—	9
door	—	—	15	sometimes	—	—	12
Episcopal	—	—	3	Springfield	—	"G" Greene County Seat	6
explain	—	"f" describe	1	stand	—	—	20
lemon	lemonade	—	2	struck	—	—	11
light	bright, clear	—	4	sugar	sweet	—	2
Lutheran	—	"L"	3	tonight	—	now + night	13
may	let, allow	—	13	turn	—	—	4
maybe	possibly, perhaps	—	10	use	—	"U"	13
				window	—	—	14

Word Drills

Lesson 11 ("ie" words)

bier, died, fiery, lied, client, piece, pierce, tier, wierd, vizier.

101 102 103 104 105 106 107 108 109 110

R-on-L

1. **Would** **you** **please** **sit** **down** **?**
"WD"

2X

2. **Be careful** **or** **you** **will** **fall.**
"V" + keep twice   stand, then fall

                                        R-on-L   WA

3. **You** **say** **you** **are** **right** **but** **I**
                                  just, correct

C-C-W

think **you** **are** **wrong.**   4. **I**
                          "Y" below chin
                          mistake

R   R-in-L   R-in-L

won't **do** **that** **lesson.**
refuse   message,
                                     sermon

  C-C-W

5. **We**   **thought**   **we**   **would**   **win**
          think   get + wave flag

WA   R-in-L

that   **game**   **but**   **we**   **lost!**
       challenge

WA   R   R-in-L
                             2X

6. **The***   **flag**   **is**   **sometimes**   **called**   **"the***
                               once in   named
                               a while

R   R   R
                                     WA

red,   **white,**   **and**   **blue"!**
lips   shirt
          open "5" hand

                                   R

7. **John**   **had**   **a**   **yellow**   **shirt,**   **a**
                               "Y"

* OPTIONAL

WA R

blue **coat,** **and** **a** **green** **tie.**
"B"   "G"

R-in-L R-in-L R   R
             WA

8. **Some** **spring** **flowers** **are** **purple.**
 part   grow   smell   "P"

9. **Most** **trees** **have** **black** **bark.**
   "5" hand   eyebrow

10. **Do** **you** **like** **pink** **lemonade** **?**
     prefer "P" on lips "L" at chin

     R-on-L   R

11. **They** **painted** **their** **house** **white**
   paint back and forth   shirt open "5" hand

                L↓ ↓R

with

R

brown
''B'' down R cheek

trim.

12. **The***

F→R

clouds

are

gray

today.
now - day

13. **Would**
''Wd''

you

R

like
prefer

to*

R-in-L

ride
in a car

R

with

me

?

14. **Do**

you

like
prefer

to*

R-on-L

ride
a horse

?

WA
BHA

15. **Turn**

R→L

left

* OPTIONAL

87

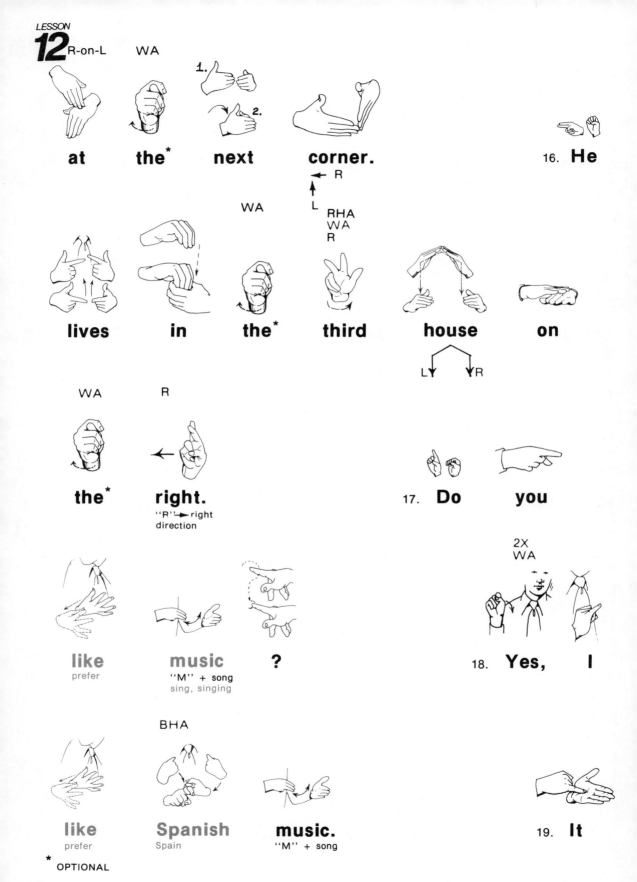

WA

1.

2.

at   **the** *   **next**   **corner.**

16. **He**

← R

↑
L   RHA
WA
R

WA

lives   **in**   **the** *   **third**   **house**   **on**

L↓   ↓R

WA   R

the *   **right.**

"R" → right
direction

17. **Do**   **you**

2X
WA

like   **music**   **?**
prefer   "M" + song
       sing, singing

18. **Yes,**   **I**

BHA

like   **Spanish**   **music.**
prefer   Spain   "M" + song

19. **It**

* OPTIONAL

R-in-L   R-on-L

is   **time**   **to***   **start**   **working.**

wrist watch   begin   labor,
job

                WA   WA

20. **Do**   **you**   **have**   **the***   **keys**   **to**

BHA

my   **car**   **?**

      drive

WORD	SYNONYM	MEMORY AID	SENTENCE	WORD	SYNONYM	MEMORY AID	SENTENCE
black	—	eyebrow	9	flag	—	—	6
blue	—	"B"	6, 7	game	challenge	—	5
brown	—	"B" down R cheek	11	green	—	"G"	7
careful	—	"V" + keep (twice)	2	keys	—	—	20
				left (turn)	—	—	15
clouds	—	—	12	lemonade	—	"L" at chin	10
fall	—	stand, then fall	2	lost (game)	—	—	5
				music	—	"M" + song	17

*
OPTIONAL

painted	—	hand is brush	11
pink	—	"P" on lips	10
purple	—	"P"	8
red	—	lips	6
ride	—	—	13
right (direction)	—	"R" R	16
right (correct)	—	—	3
sit (down)	—	—	1
Spanish	Spain	—	18

start	—	—	19
third	—	—	16
trees	—	"5" hand	9
white	—	shirt	6,11
win	—	get + wave flag	5
won't	refuse	—	4
wrong	mistake	"Y" below chin	3
yellow	—	—	7

Word Drills

Lesson 12 ("oe" words)

aloes, coerce, foe, doer, doe, moe, hoe, Joe, poem, noes, shoes, toes, poet, roe, woes.

111 112 113 114 115 116 117 118 119 120

R-on-L

WA   WA   R-in-L

1. **Stop**   **at**   **the***   **store**
      sell,
      sales,
      shops
   and   **buy**

R-on-L   R
            WA

me   **some**
     part
   bread,   **fish,**   **melons,**   **and**

R-in-L

bananas.   2. **It**   **is**   **warm**
           blowing on hand
   in

2X

this   **room.**   3. **I**   **like**   **it**
now   prefer

BHA

better   **when**   **it**   **is**   **cool**   **in**

 L   R

* OPTIONAL

the *

house.

L ↓ ↘R

4. **"Are**

you

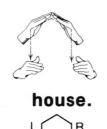

sick?"
head
stomach

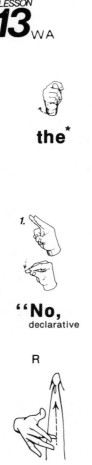

1.

"No,
declarative

I

am

well."
healthy

5. **I**

R

R-in-L

R

WA

felt
up chest

1.
2.

weak

yesterday,

but

am

strong
muscle
strength

now.

6. **It**

doesn't matter
although,
anyway

to

me,

but

I

wish
want,
desire
long for

you

were

* OPTIONAL

BHA
OUT
AA

F → R

going

too.
also

7. **I** **am** **thirsty**
down throat

R

R

and **hungry.**
down chest

8. **I** **will** **get**

you **a** **drink**
glass **of** **water.**
"W" at mouth

BHA

BHA
OUT
AA

9. **When** **I** **visited**
"V" out **their** **home**
eat-sleep **I**

L ↓ ↓ R

R

R

WA

saw **rats**
"R"
touch nose **and** **mice.**
forefinger like "rats"
touch nose

10. **The***

* OPTIONAL

rooster
"3" at forehead

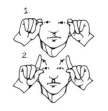

awakened
woke up

us

R-on-L

early

in

WA

the*

R

morning.
sun comes up

11. **I**

heard
"C" at ear

the*

owl

screaming
shouting

all

night.

12. **He**

read

us

stories

from

Greece
"G" at bridge of nose

and

Rome.
"R" at bridge of nose

13. **He**

C-C-W

who

IN

comes

from

*
OPTIONAL

C-C-W

Africa
"A" C-C-W
in front of face

appreciates
likes,
pleases,
pleasure,
enjoy

America.
rail fence

14. **How**

R-in-L

did **that**

WA

happen

?

WA

15. **The***

F→L

man

hated
snap fingers out

WA

the*

cold

and

the*

2.

1.

snow.
white rain

16. **He**

is

an

eager
enthusiastic,
anxious

1.

2.

worker,

WA

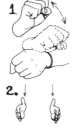

but

R

stubborn.
mule

17. **They**

were

WA
BHA

quarreling,
cock fights

* OPTIONAL

WA

R-on-L

but   **I**   **stood**   **between**   **them**   **and**

R-in-L   R-in-L

stopped   **it.**   18. **Don't**   **bother**   **me**
                          Not

BHA
AA

when   **I**   **am**   **talking!**   19. **You**

CW   R-in-L

always   **interrupt**   **me!**   20. **Will**

R-in-L

you   **print**   **this**   **program**   **for**   **me**   **?**
      newspaper   "P"

WORD	SYNONYM	MEMORY AID	SENTENCE	WORD	SYNONYM	MEMORY AID	SENTENCE
Africa	—	"A"-C-C-W in front of face	13	morning	—	sun comes up	10
America	—	—	13	owl	—	—	11
appreciates	like, pleases, pleasure, enjoy	—	13	print	newspaper	—	20
				program	—	"P"	20
				quarreling	—	cock fights	17
awakened	woke	woke up	10	rats	—	"R"	9
bananas	—	—	1	Rome	—	"R" at bridge of nose	12
between	—	—	17				
bother	—	—	18	rooster	—	"3" at forehead	10
bread	—	—	1				
cool	—	—	3	screaming	shouting	—	11
doesn't matter	although, anyway	—	6	sick	—	head, stomach	4
				snow	—	white rain	15
eager	enthusiastic, anxious	—	16	stop	—	—	1, 17
				store	sell, sales, shops	—	1
fish	—	—	1				
Greece	—	"G" at bridge of nose	12	strong	strength	muscle	5
				stubborn	mule	—	16
hated	—	—	15	thirsty	—	down throat	7
hungry	—	down chest	7	water	—	"W" at mouth	8
interrupt	—	—	19				
melons	—	—	1	weak	—	—	5
mice	—	forefinger like "rats"	9	well	—	—	4
				wish	want, desire, long for	—	6

Word Drills

Lesson 13 ("qu" words)

quad, quiz, quick, quack, equal, quill, equate, squawk, square, quorum, sequel, quarry, squall, mosque, squalid, acquire, quarter, quantity, quizzical, quake.

121 122 123 124 125 126 127 128 129 130

1. Many

hearing
speaking,
say,
tell

BHA
AA

people
"P"s

are

R

ignorant
"V" on forehead

CW

about

WA

the*

deaf.
ear + closed

C-C-W

2. The*

reason
"R" on forehead

R

for   **this**
now

is

they

R

misunderstand
mean, intend on forehead

R-O-L

each   other.
fellowship,
stir,
one
another

3. We

R

must
need,
should,
have to,
ought to

R

be careful   not   to*
"V"s, sign "keep" twice

2X

complain
gripe,
grumble

CW

about

*
OPTIONAL

98

them.

4. **Would** **you**

please
like,
prefer,
enjoy,
pleasure

bake
cook

me

R-in-L

some

R-in-L

cookies,

a

R-in-L

cake,

and,

R-in-L

a **pie** **?**

5. **I**

would
"WD"

R-in-L

like

some

R-on-L

bread,

R-in-L

butter,

and

doughnuts.

6. **Do**

you

like

a

little

milk

in

your

R-in-L

tea

?

R-on-l

7. **I**

like

vinegar
"V" at mouth

on

my

salad

with

salt

and

pepper.

8. **He**

R

smelled

R

strongly

of

whiskey

(vodka).
"V" on back of hand

9. **Can**
Able

she

cook

a

good

R-in-L

meal

?

R-in-L

10. **His**   **new**   **home**   **has**   **a**   **living**

eat, sleep

room,   **dining**   **room,**   **kitchen,**   **bathroom,**   **and**

eating   cook

R-on-L

three   **bedrooms.**   11. **I**   **sat**   **at**

sit,
chair

WA

the*   **table**   **and**   **dropped**   **my**   **napkin.**

"B" across mouth

R-on-L   R

12. **The***   **coffee**   **was**   **sweet,**   **but**   **the***

sugar

* OPTIONAL

R-on-L

chocolate
"C"
milk
was
sour.
bitter
13. **Do**

2X

you
like
prefer
corn
and
cabbage
with

R

nuts
and
bacon
?
14. **Don't**
Not

R-in-L

bother
me,
I
am
too
busy.
business

WF

WA

15. **He**
is
idle
vacation
most
of
the*
time.
wrist,
watch

* OPTIONAL

102

R

I   **say**
tell,
speak
   he   **is**   **lazy.**
"L" on L shoulder
   16. **I**

F→R

doubt   **if**   **he**   **really**   **has**   **as**

F→R

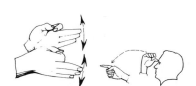

much
amount
   money   **as**   **he**   **says.**
tells,
speaks

WA   R-on-L

17. **The***   **ring**
"R"
   looks
appears,
seems
   cheap,   **but**   **he**

R-in-L

said
say,
tell
   it   **was**   **expensive.**   18. **One**

* OPTIONAL

R

day   **it**   **is**   **dry**   **here,**   **and**   **the***

R-on-L

1.
2.

next   **day**   **it**   **is**   **wet.**
soft,
tender,
gentle

1.
2.

R   R

19. **We**   **took**   **a**   **true,**   **false**   **test.**
speak from   questions, many
side of mouth

20. **He**   **is**   **a**   **liar.**
lie + person

* OPTIONAL

104

WORD	SYNONYM	MEMORY AID	SENTENCE	WORD	SYNONYM	MEMORY AID	SENTENCE
bacon	—	—	13	lazy	—	"L" on L shoulder	15
bake	cook	—	4	liar	—	lie + person	20
bathroom	—	—	10	little	—	—	6
bedroom	—	—	10	milk	—	—	6, 12
busy	business	—	14	misunderstand	—	mean, intend on forehead	2
butter	—	—	5
cabbage	—	—	13	napkin	—	"B" across mouth	11
cake	—	—	4
cheap	—	—	17	nuts	—	—	13
chocolate	—	"C"	12	pepper	—	—	7
complain	gripe, grumble	—	3	pie	—	—	4
				really	—	—	16
cook	—	—	9	reason	—	"R" on forehead	2
cookies	—	—	4
corn	—	—	13	ring	—	"R"	17
doubt	—	—	16	salt	—	—	7
doughnuts	—	—	5	smelled	—	—	8
drop	—	—	11	sour	bitter	—	12
dry	—	—	18	sweet	sugar	—	12
each (other)	fellowship, stir, one another	—	2	test	—	questions, many	19
expensive	—	—	17	vinegar	—	"V" at mouth	7
idle	vacation	—	15	wet	soft, tender gentle	—	18
ignorant	—	"V" on forehead	1
				whiskey	—	—	8
kitchen	cook	—	10

Word Drills

Lesson 14 ("om" words)

bomb, comb, home, boom, romp, some, tome, Nome, axiom, momma, mommy, vomit, woman, foment, pompom, domestic.

131 132 133 134 135 136 137 138 139 140

1.  **His** **friend**
hooked forefingers **is** **very**
"V" hands **intelligent**
center finger from
forehead **(smart).**
forefinger

R-in-L

2. **What** **time**
wrist watch   **did** **you** **arrive** **?**

F→R   OUT

3. **I** **am**  **planning** **to**[*] **visit**
"V"'s **my**

 **mother** **and**  **father.** 4. **I**

OUT

 enjoy
prefer,
like **traveling** **with** **my** **assistant**
"A" support

 * OPTIONAL

manager.
master

5. **I**

would
"WD"

rather
better

take

F→L

WA

R-on-L

a

plane

than

the *

train

or

bus.

R-on-L

6. **I**

almost
barely

missed

the *

train.

7. **The** *

multiplication
worse

test
questions,
many

was

easy.
simple

8. **He**

has

a lot of
much

responsibility.
2 "R" on R shoulder

* OPTIONAL

9. **To**[*]   **obey**   **is**   **better**   **than**   **to**[*]

disobey.   10. **I**   **have**   **a**   **great**
"L"

R►L   OUT

burden   **to**[*]   **carry.**   11. **I**   **visited**
open hands,   "V"'s
like responsibility

R   R

a   **farm**   **and**   **saw**   **a**   **horse,**   **mule,**
"5" hand under
chin

R   WA

cow,   **goats,**   **and**   **sheep.**   12. **The**[*]
"Y"   chin, forehead   cut wool

1.
2.

next **evening**
night

we

went

OUT

downtown
town

on

BHA

1.
2.

our **bicycles.**
pedaling

13. **I** **have** **visited**
"V"s

C-C-W

Japan,
"J" at eye

Korea
"K" at eye

and **the** **Philipines.**
"F" at nose

14. **I** **would**
"Wd"

like
prefer

you

to *

stay
continue

with

R-in-L
2X

me

as

often
again & again

as

you

can.
able,
could

* OPTIONAL

CW
   F➤R

15. **We**   **agree**   **about**   **so**   **many**   **things,**
think-same

    CW

but   **I**   **disagree**   **with**   **you**   **about**
think-opposite

BHA
AA

this.   16. **If**   **you**   **continue**
now   stay
still

to***   **quarrel**   **with**   **me**   **I**   **will**
cock fight

R

become   **angry.**   17. **I**   **see**   **you**
wrath,
anger

*
OPTIONAL

110

CW

are   **very**   **calm**   **about**   **it.**
        "V" hands   quiet

R

18. **I**   **understand**   **you**   **do   not**   **accept**

R-ın-L

criticism   **easily.**   19. **I**   **respect**
cancel   simple   "R"

you,   **but**   **I**   **cannot**   **honor**   **you.**
                                              "H"

R-U-L

20. **He**   **is**   **a**   **humble**   **man**   **who**
                                      meek

can   **stand**   **pressure.**

WORD	SYNONYM	MEMORY AID	SENTENCE
accept	—	—	18
agree	—	think - same	15
almost	barely	—	6
angry	wrath, anger	—	16
assistant	—	"A" + support	4
bicycles	—	pedaling	12
burden	—	open hands, like responsibility	10
calm	quiet	—	17
continue	stay	—	16
cow	—	—	11
criticism	—	—	18
disagree	—	think - opposite	15
disobey	—	—	9
downtown	town	—	12
easy	simple	—	7, 18
farm	—	"5" hand under chin	11

WORD	SYNONYM	MEMORY AID	SENTENCE
goats	—	chin, forehead	11
honor	—	—	19
horse	—	—	11
humble	—	—	20
intelligent	—	center finger from forehead	1
Japan	—	"J" at eye	13
Korea	—	"K" at eye	13
manager	master	—	4
mule	—	—	11
multiplication	multiply, worse	—	7
obey	—	—	9
Philippines	—	"F" at nose	13
pressure	—	—	20
respect	—	—	19
responsibility	—	2 "R"'s on R shoulder	8
sheep	—	cut wool	11
train	—	—	5, 6
traveling	trip	—	4

Word Drills

Lesson 15 ("on" words)

aeons, bone, cone, done, eons, neon, fondle, gone, honest, lion, wrong, ikon, long, among, hone, dipthong, pong, tong, avon, soon, tone, won, yonder, son.

141 142 143 144 145 146 147 148 149 150

1. **His** **brother** **is** **very** **proud** **of**
pride

WA

him. 2. **The*** **car** **passed**
"A" hand passes L ➤ R

F ➤ R   AA   R-in-L

us **as** **if** **in** **a** **race.**
compete

AA   WF

3. **If** **you** **would** **study** **more**
"WD"

2X
BHA   F ➤ R

you **could** **succeed** **too!**
do second time higher   also

* OPTIONAL

WA   R-on-L   R

4. **You**   **have**   **the***   **right**   **idea!**

         R   R

5. **You**   **should**
    need,
    etc.   **not**   **let**   **your**   **imagination**
        allow

AA   WF

control   **your**   **life.**   6. **College**
rule,   school + over
reign,
master

                                       F→R

requires   **you**   **to***   **memorize**   **many**   **things.**
requirement,   mind-grasp
insists,
requests

       C-C-W

7. **My**   **reason**   **for**   **telling**   **you**   **this**
       "R" like think   saying,   now
                          speaking

*
OPTIONAL

L-in-R
2.

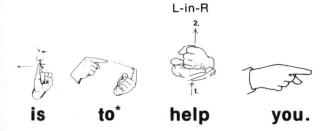

is **to*** **help** **you.** 8. **Do**

F➤L

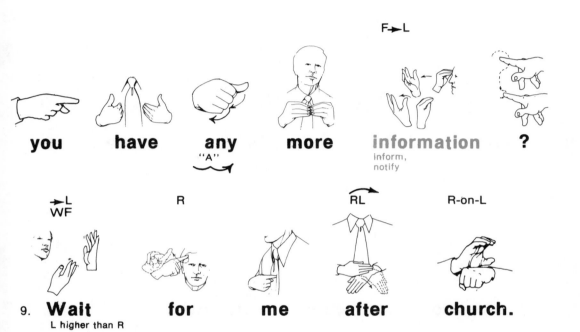

you **have** **any** **more** **information** **?**
"A" inform,
notify

➤L
WF

R RL R-on-L

9. **Wait** **for** **me** **after** **church.**
L higher than R

OUT R-in-L

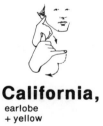

10. **I** **have** **visited** **California,** **New** **York,**
"V" earlobe "Y" in L palm ◄──►
+ yellow

Chicago, **and** **Detroit.** 11. **I**
"C" "D"

*
OPTIONAL

115

OUT   R   CW   CW

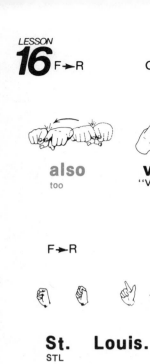

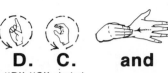

also   **visited**   **Washington,**   **D.   C.**   **and**
too   "V"'s   "W" R shoulder out   "D" "C" circled

F→R   R

→ R

St.   Louis.   12. **While**   **there**   **I**
STL   during

OUT   WA

visited   **the***   **Lincoln**   **Memorial.**
"V"'s   "L" on forehead

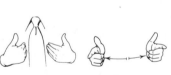

13. **I**   **believe**   **Lincoln**   **had**   **great**   **principles.**
                mind + clasp   "L" on forehead   R "P" in L palm
                trust   facing out.

14. **In**   **our**   **generation**   **we**   **read**   **of**

L   R

* OPTIONAL

116

2X

divorces
"D"

daily.
"A" brushes R cheek twice

15. **In a few days**
tomorrow + few

R-in-L

R-on-L

we

will

begin

regular
"just" twice

classes.
"C"

16. **A few days ago**
yesterday + few

I

was

asked
prayed

a

foolish
"Y"
silly,
ridiculous

question.
?

17. **It**

is

a

R

wise

person
2 "P"'s

who
whom

does not

believe
mind + grasp
trust

in

dreams.

R forehead → R

18. **He**

 **was**

stupid

back of "V"
on forehead

compared

cupped hands

to*

his

brother.

male + same

19. **I**

was

surprised

eyes snap open

R

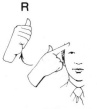

because

R

his **idea**

was

judged

decision

best.

20. **I**

suspect

scratch forehead

R-O-L IN

he

received

attention

horse blinders

R

because

he

* OPTIONAL

was

so

careless.
"V" like foolish

WORD	SYNONYM	MEMORY AID	SENTENCE
a few days ago	—	yesterday + few	16
attention	—	horse blinders	20
believe	trust	mind + clasp	13
California	—	earlobe + yellow	10
Chicago	—	"C"	10
compared	—	cupped hands	18
control	rule, reign, master	—	5
daily	—	"A" brushes R cheek twice	14
Detroit	—	"D"	10
divorces	—	"D"	14
dreams	—	R forehead-R	17
foolish	ridiculous, silly	"Y"	16
idea	—	—	4
imagination	—	—	5
in a few days	—	tomorrow + few	15
information	inform, notify	—	8
judged	decision	—	19
life	—	—	5
Lincoln	—	"L" on forehead	12, 13
memorize	—	mind - grasp	6
New York	—	"Y" in L palm	10

WORD	SYNONYM	MEMORY AID	SENTENCE
passed	—	"A" hand passes L ➞ R	2
principles	—	R "P" in L palm facing out	13
proud	pride	—	1
question	—	?	16
received	—	—	20
regular	—	just	15
requires	requirement, insists, requests	—	6
study	—	—	3
stupid	—	back of "V" on forehead	18
succeed	—	—	3
surprised	—	—	19
suspect	—	—	20
things	—	—	6
wait	—	L higher than R	9
Washington, D.C.	—	"W" on R shoulder-out "D", "C" circled	11
while	during	➞	12
wise	—	—	17

Word Drills

Lesson 16 ("an" and "er" words)

another, antique, wander, sander, than, anthology, pander, either, neither, other, brother, German, mother, ere.

151 152 153 154 155 156 157 158 159 160

R-O-L

1. **My** **advice** **to** **him** **was** **to***

R-in-L   IN

stop **deceiving** **people.**   2. **His**
dealing under the table   "P"s

R-O-L   WA   R-in-L

influence **in** **the*** **class** **proved** **he**
large advice   "C"

didn't   care.   3. **He** **invented**
                    "4" hand up from
                    forehead

C-C-W

his **reason** **for** **missing** **class.**
      "R" like think

* OPTIONAL

4. **I**   **guess**   **he**   **is**   **just**   **crazy.**

''5'' claw hand
at R ear rotated.

RL

5. **She**   **became**   **dizzy**   **after**   **he**   **kissed**

      L-in front R   ''5'' claw hand   mouth-cheek

               in front of eyes

her.   6. **It**   **is**   **comfortable**   **to***

know   **he**   **doesn't want**   **to get even.**

          want + dump out   get revenge

7. **He**   **is**   **so**   **selfish**   **that**   **I**   **really**

          ''3'' hands towards hips

* OPTIONAL

pity
mercy

him.

WA

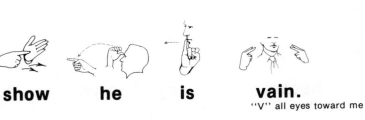

8. **His**

jealousy
envy
"J"

and

BHA
AA

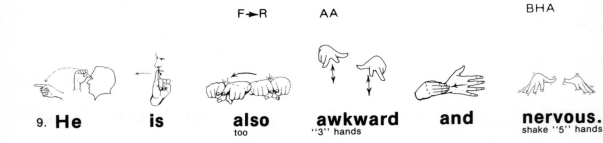

boasting   **show**   **he**   **is**   **vain.**
"V" all eyes toward me

F→R   AA   BHA

9. **He**   **is**   **also**   **awkward**   **and**   **nervous.**
too   "3" hands   shake "5" hands

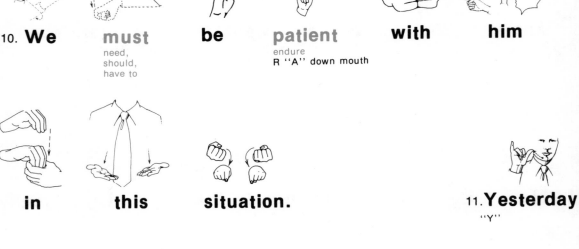

10. **We**   **must**   **be**   **patient**   **with**   **him**
need,   endure
should,   R "A" down mouth
have to

in   **this**   **situation.**   11.**Yesterday**
"Y"

he   **was**   **ashamed**   **and**   **embarrassed.**
red and flushed face

→L   R-on-L

12. **He**   **causes**   **much**   **grief**   **and**   **suffering**
a lot of,   "A" hands-crushed   "S" hands around
amount   heart   each other

BHA

to   **his**   **mother.**   13. **He**

is   **really**   **discouraged**   **and**   **cries**   **because**
"R"   "V"   tears flowing

R

he   **is**   **lonely.**   14. **I**   **was**

*
OPTIONAL

WA

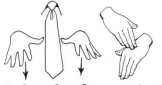
shocked
"5" hands

at

the*

amount

of

pain
nerves jangle

he

could
able,
can

bear.

15 **They**

had
must,
need,
should

to*

WA

separate

the*

girls
female - small

from

the*

boys.
male - small

16.**What**

goes

up

must
need,
should,
have to

come

down.

R-in-L

WA

17. **He**

stood

before
in the presence of,
presence

the*

judge
decision + person

* OPTIONAL

124

2X

and **pleaded** **innocent.** 18. **We**
begged two ''H''s on lips,
then out

→ R

 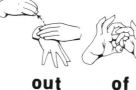 

went **out** **of** **town** **ahead** **of**
go roof tops

→ R

others. 19. **We** **saw** **him** **among**

WA IN

the* **people,** **then** **he** **suddenly**
''P'' hands quickly,
immediately

WA

disappeared. 20. **I** **was** **in** **the***
vanished, solved problem

* OPTIONAL

→ R

R-in-L

center **of** **town** **when** **my** car **stopped.**
"M"   rooftops   drive

WORD	SYNONYM	MEMORY AID	SENTENCE	WORD	SYNONYM	MEMORY AID	SENTENCE
advice	—	—	1	guess	—	—	4
ahead of	—	—	18	influence	—	large advice	2
among	—	—	19	innocent	—	two "H"s on lips, then out	17
amount	—	—	14	invented	—	"4" hand-up from forehead	3
ashamed	—	—	11				
awkward	—	"3" hands	9	jealousy	envy	"J"	8
became		L in front of R	5	kissed	—	mouth - cheek	5
before	in the presence of	—	17	lonely	—	—	13
				nerves	—	shake "5" hands	9
boasting	—	—	8	pain	—	nerve jangle	14
causes	—	—	12	patient	endure	—	10
center	—	"M"	20	pity	mercy	—	7
comfortable	—	—	6	pleaded	begged	—	17
deceiving	—	dealing under the table	1	proved	—	—	2
				to get even	get revenge	—	6
didn't care	—	—	2	selfish	—	"3" hands toward hips	7
disappeared	vanished, solved problem	—	19				
				separate	—	—	15
discouraged	—	"V"	13	shocked	—	"5" hands	14
dizzy	—	"5" "claw" hand in front of eyes C-C-W	5	show	—	—	8
				situation	—	—	10
doesn't want	—	want + dump out	6	suddenly	quickly, immediately	—	19
down	—	—	16	suffering	—	"S" hands around each other	12
embarrassed	—	red and flushed face	11				
grief	—	"A" hands crushed heart	12	up	—	—	16
				vain	—	all eyes toward me	8

Word Drills

Lesson 17 ("ar" words)

Aaron, Adar, Archelaus, Archippus, Artemas, Barak, Potiphar, Pharaoh, Barabbas, Barnabas, Darius, Hagar, Mary, Mark, Omar.

161 162 163 164 165 166 167 168 169 170

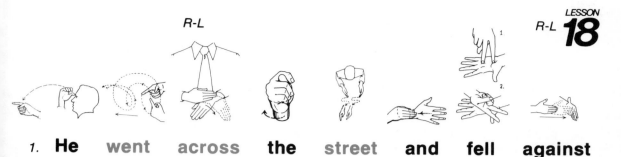

1. **He**   **went**   **across**   **the**   **street**   **and**   **fell**   **against**
    go   after   way

a   **high**   **wall.**

2. **We**   **believe**   **in**   **the**   **resurrection**
    trust   get-up

$F \rightarrow R$

from   **death.**
   turn over→R

3. **Will**   **you**   **please**   **lie down**
    like   R "V" in L
    enjoy
    pleasure

R-in-L   R-on-L

and   **stop**   **jumping?**

4. **We**   **were**   **at**   **a**   **party**
    "P" like play

R-in-L   WA   R-on-L

where   **we**   **had to**   **kneel**   **all**   **the**   **time.**
     should
     must
     need

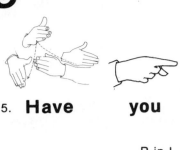

5. **Have** **you** **traveled** **much** **?**
amount,
lot of

R-in-L   WA

6. **While** **in** **the*** **Army,** **we** **had** **to**
need
must
should
ought

F→L   BHA / AA   R-U-L → R

march, **climb,** **and** **run** **without** **rest.**
"R"

7. **He** **finally** **overcame** **his** **habit** **of**
finished,
already
    mind + bound

WF   R

flirting.   8. **A** **stray** **cat** **hurried**
off the track   whiskers

* OPTIONAL

128

RL

across
after

WA

the*   **street.**

9. **John**

F→L

led

in

WA

the*

R-U-L→R

escape

attempt.
try
"T"

10. **We**   **were**   **told**
say,
speak

to   **line**   **up**
"5" hands

and   **wait**

L
WF

WA

for   **the***   **train.**
tracks

11. **It**   **is**

R-in-L   R-in-L

important
valuable, special

that   **we**   **be**   **born**   **again.**

* OPTIONAL

12. **The***   food   **tasted**   **and**   **smelled**   terrible,

     eat   awful,
                                                                    horrible

2X

but   **he**   **was**   **polite.**   13. **As**

                                        like ''fine''

      R-on-L   WA

I   **touched**   **the***   meat,   **I**   **noticed**

                                  flesh   from eye to L palm

                                                                        WA

that   **it**   **was**   **spoiled.**   14. **The***

                                     ruined

                                                R-in-L

salesman   **was**   trying   **to***   **impress**   **us**

                        attempt
                        ''T''

* OPTIONAL

R-in-L

as   **he**   **arrived.**

15. **Jesus**

R   R

said
tell,
say

we

should
need,
must,
have to

deny
push down
desires

ourselves.
our + self

16. **He**   **accused**
blamed,
at fault,
condemn

me   **of**   **stealing,**   **but**

BHA
AA

WA

I   **denied**
not, not

it.

17. **The***   **person**
"P"'s

BHA
AA

F➤R   R-in-L

who
whom

truly

serves
carry

will

also
too

share

*** OPTIONAL**

all   **he**   **has.**

18. **I**   **warned**

WA

him   **not**   **to***   **leave**   **the***   **room.**

"R" hands

WA

19. **Are**   **you**   **coming**   **to**   **the***   **meeting**
                                     come   service,
                                                                                   gathering

                              R-on-L
                                                                            2X

?   20. **He**   **scattered**   **paper**

C-C-W

around   **the***   **room.**

*****OPTIONAL

WORD	SYNONYM	MEMORY AID	SENTENCE		WORD	SYNONYM	MEMORY AID	SENTENCE
accused	blamed, at fault	—	16		led	—	—	9
across	after	—	1, 8		lie down	—	R "V" in L	3
against	—	—	1		line up	—	"5" hands	10
army	—	—	6		march	—	—	6
attempt	—	"T" (try)	9		noticed	—	from eye to L palm	13
born	—	—	11		ourselves	—	our + self	15
climb	—	—	6		overcame	—	—	7
death	dead	turn over ➤ R	2		polite	—	like "fine"	12
denied	—	not, not	16		rest	—	"R"	6
deny	—	push down desires	15		resurrection	—	get up	2
					salesman	—	—	14
escape	—	—	9		scattered	—	—	20
finally	finished, already	—	7		serves	—	carry tray	17
					share	—	—	17
flirting	—	—	7		spoiled	ruined	—	13
food	eat	—	12		stealing	—	—	16
high	—	—	1		stray	—	off the track	8
hurried	—	"H"	8		street	way	—	1, 8
important	valuable, special	—	11		tasted	—	—	12
					terrible	awful, horrible	—	12
impress	—	—	14					
jumping	—	—	3		touched	—	—	13
kneel	—	—	4		trying	attempt	"T"	14
					warned	—	—	18

Word Drills

Lesson 18 ("mixed" words)

Abednego, Edom, Obed, Tobiah, Sarah, Noah, Obadiah, Orpah, Pekah, Rahab, Terah, Abraham, Adah, Adonijah, Ahab, Ahaz, Delilah.

171 172 173 174 175 176 177 178 179 180

1. **He** **told**
say, speak
us **we** **could** **choose,**

RHA

but **instead**
substitute, except
he **appointed** **Mr.** **Smith.**

R-in-L

R-on-L

2. **Show**
example
me **some**
part
of **your** **work.**
job, labor

3. **Give** **me** **an** **example** **to***
explain
describe
"F" hands

R-in-L

that.

4. **I** **offered**
suggest, present
to* **change**
modified "A"
hands

*OPTIONAL

134

1.
2.

interpreters
"F" hands

because

of

WA

the*

vocabulary.
"V" like word

5. **I**

volunteered
applied, as for a job

to*

postpone
to put off, delay

WA

the*

2X

punishment.

BHA

WA

6. **They**

surrendered
gave us, yielded

rather
better

than

defend

the*

city.
rooftops

·7. **Did**

you

EA
BHA
OUT

visit
"V"

his

grave
mound of soil
over grave, bury

yet
late

?

8. **He**

tried
"T"

*** OPTIONAL**

135

R-U-L

to*   **hide**   **what**   **he**   **stole,**   **but**   **he**

was   **to***   **blame.**
at fault
accuse

9. **Will**   **you**

L-in-R   R-on-L

help   **establish**   **a**   **home**   **for**   **those**   **who**

are   **tempted**   **to***   **steal**   **?**
temptation   up the sleeve.

10. **I**   **fail**   **to***   **understand**   **why**   **they**
     "V" of L palm   light goes on   "Y"

***** OPTIONAL

WA

have **the*** **urge**
tug, draw **to*** **steal.**
up the sleeve.

11. **If**
"F"

WF

you **study** **their** **ways**
"W" **I** **am** **sure**
true

you **can**
could,
able R-in-L
count C-C-W
many **reasons.**
"R" as think

CW   CW

12. **Did** **you** **graduate**
"G" in L palm **from** **high school**
"H" "S" circled CW **?**

13. **Your** **skill**
experience **in** **interpreting**
"F" hands **is** **improving.**
R on L up arm

* OPTIONAL

R-in-L

14. **His** sermon **was** **so** **expanded** **that**
   lesson

it needed **to** **be** **condensed.**
must, should,
have to

BHA

15. **I** cannot **measure** **how** much **he**
   can't   "Y"s   amount

R-in-L

earns. 16. **I** **know** **he** spends
                                           buys

WA   2X   R-on-L

all the* **money** **he** **borrows** **and**
                                   "V" hands in

*OPTIONAL

R-on-L

lends **to** **no one.**
"V" hands out

R-on-L

17. **He** **just**
right
correct

R-on-L
OUT

2X
R-in-L

cannot **save** **enough** **money** **for** **it.**
can't   store, reserve
"V" back of
"s", $,

2X

WA

18. **I** **begged** **him** **to*** **deliver** **the***
plead   bring

R-on-L

WA

newspaper **free** **of** **charge.** 19. **The***
linotype   "F"   cost
fine

WA

president **had to** **break** **the*** **vote** **to***
need, etc. break stick   ballot in box

* OPTIONAL

139

cooperate.
gears mesh together

20. **He**   finally   forbade
             last, final   negative

 → R   L ➤ B   WA

anyone   **to***   **leave**   **the***   **room.**

WORD	SYNONYM	MEMORY AID	SENTENCE
anyone	—	—	20
appointed	—	—	1
because	—	—	4
begged	plead	—	18
blame	at fault	—	8
cannot	—	—	15,17
change	—	modified "A" hands	4
charge	cost	—	18
choose	—	—	1
city	—	roof tops	6
condensed	—	—	14
cooperate	—	gears mesh together	19
count	—	—	11
defend	—	—	6
deliver	bring	—	18
earns	—	—	15
establish	—	—	9
example	—	—	3
expand	—	—	14
fail	—	"V" off L palm	10
forbid	negative	—	20
free	—	"F"	18
graduate	—	"G" in L	12

WORD	SYNONYM	MEMORY AID	SENTENCE
grave	—	mound of soil over grave	7
hide	—	—	8
high school	—	"H" & "S" circled	12
improving	—	R on L up arm	13
instead	except, substitute	—	1
interpreters	—	"F" hands	4
interpreting	—	"F" hands	13
lends	—	"V" hands out	16
measure	—	"Y"s	15
offered	suggest, present	—	4
postpone	to put off, delay	—	5
punishment	—	—	5
sermon	lesson	—	14
skill	experience	—	13
spends	buys	—	16
surrender	give up. yielded	—	6
tempted	—	—	9
urge	—	tug, draw	10
vocabulary	—	"V" like "Word"	14
volunteered	—	—	5
vote	—	ballot in box	19
ways	—	"W"	11

Word Drills

Lesson 19 ("ah" words)

Dinah, Elijah, Jonah, Leah, Josiah, Judah, Korah.

181 182 183 184 185 186 187 188 189 190

* OPTIONAL

1.

I **like**
prefer **him,** **but** **you** **can't**
cannot **depend**

on * **him.** 2. **If** **I** **have**
prefer
must,
should
etc.

R-in-L

RHA
OUT

to * **I** **will** **force**
"C" forward **you** **to** * **stop**

teasing
slight persecution **him.** 3. **You** **can** **depend**

R-U-L → UP

AA

on * **my** **support.** 4. **He** **rules**
controls,
reigns

*
OPTIONAL

R-on-L

with   **an**   **iron**   **hand.**   5. **I**

"I"

have   **some**   **ironing**   **and**   **sewing**   **to**   **do.**

     part

R-in-L

6. **Will**   **you**   **please**   **cut out**   **that**   **picture**   **?**

enjoy
like
pleasure

7. **He**   **loves**   **to**   **hunt**   **and**   **fish**   **since**

      gun   casting rod

he   **retired.**   8. **He**   **is**   **very**

 "R's" like leisure   "V"s

*
OPTIONAL

R-in-L

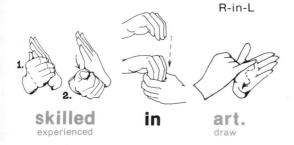

skilled   **in**   **art.**
experienced   draw

9. **Soon**   **the***
short

time   **of**   **reaping**   **will**   **be**   **over.**
"T"   harvest   completed

C-C-W

10. **He**   **is**   **hard-of-hearing,**   **but**   **lip-reads**
             "H" → "H"   speech-reads

R-on-L

better   **than**   **average.**
               medium

11. **He**   **really**
        R like true

has   **a**   **good**   **voice.**
                       "V" up throat

12. **Would**
"WD"

*
OPTIONAL

R-on-L   WA

you   **please**   **make**   **the***   **announcements**   **now**

like, enjoy   proclaim
pleasure

?   13. **She**   **has**   **a**   **bad**   **habit**

mind bound

BHA

 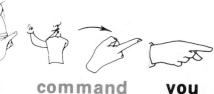

of   **gossiping.**   14. **I**   **command**   **you**

order
large tell

R-in-L   BHA   R-in-L

to*   **stop**   **doing**   **that.**   15. **I**   **told**

say
speak
tell

2X

them   **not**   **to***   **whisper**   **in**   **class.**

"C" group

*****
OPTIONAL

144

R-on-L   R   → R

16. **I   promised   not   to*   scold   him   any**

more.   17. **They   shouted   and**
                    "C" up

→ L

mocked   Jesus   before   they   killed   Him.
            nail prints

R-in-L

18. **I   wrote   a   letter   to   the*   radio   station.**

R→L

19. **The*   clouds   are   dark   today   with**
                        Black   now + day
                        + dark

thundering   and   lightning.   20. **We**

BHA
AA

walked   in   the*   valley   and   then   climbed

the*   mountain.
rock + hill

WORD	SYNONYM	MEMORY AID	SENTENCE	WORD	SYNONYM	MEMORY AID	SENTENCE
art	draw	—	8	reaping	harvest	—	9
average	medium	—	10	retired	—	"R" like leisure	7
command	order	large tell	14				
depend	—	—	1,3	rules	controls, reigns	—	4
force	—	"C" forward	2				
gossiping	—	—	13	scold	—	—	16
hard-of-hear-ing	—	"H" "H"	10	sewing	—	—	5
				shouted	—	"C" up	17
hunt	—	gun	7	since	—	—	7
iron	—	"I"	4	support	—	—	3
ironing	—	—	5	teasing	—	slight per-secution	2
killed	—	—	17				
lightning	—	—	19	thundering	—	—	19
lip-reads	speech-reads	—	10	valley	—	—	20
loves	—	—	7	voice	—	"V" up throat	11
mountain	—	rock + hill	20				
promised	—	—	16	whisper	—	—	15
radio	—	—	18				

*
OPTIONAL

Word Drills

Lesson 20 (''th'' words)

Seth, Ruth, Nathan, Nathanael, Thomas, Abiathar, Matthew, Goliath, Elizabeth, Jethro, Esther, Timothy, Dathan.

    191 192 193 194 195 196 197 198 199 200

IN

BHA
AA

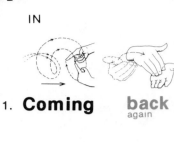

1. **Coming** **back** **we** **walked** **along** **the***
again

2X

sea **shore.** 2. **Will** **you**
waves

C-C-W

WA

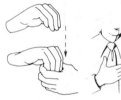

take care of **the*** **grass** **and** **flowers** **in** **my**
keep C-C-W grow + smell
green

→ L

garden **?** 3. **He** **subtracted [omitted]**
hoeing take away

R-in-L

WA

my **share** **of** **the*** **profits.** 4. **What**
money in watch
pocket

*
OPTIONAL

percent   **did**   **he**   **pay**   **you**   **after**   **they**

L ➤ R

divided   **the**   **farm**   **?**
beard

5. **He**   **looks**
appears
seems

very   **thin**   **now.**
thin cheeks

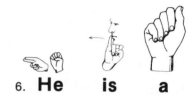

6. **He**   **is**   **a**

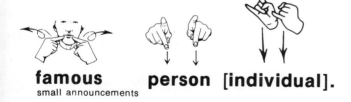

famous   **person [individual].**
small announcements

7. **He**

is   **a**   **perfect**   **gentleman**   **and**   **very**
"P"   man + ruffles

polite.
proper

8. **His**   **clothes**   **are**   **always**

R-in-L

smooth.
thumb across
fingertips

9. **Is**   **that**   **knife**   **sharp**

R-U-L

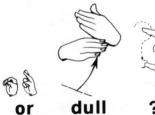

or   **dull**   **?**

10. **My**   **best**   **friend**
locked
forefingers

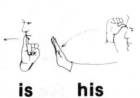 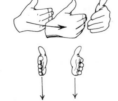

is   **his**   **neighbor.**
near person

11. **Do**   **you**

have   **a**   **sweetheart**   **?**

12. **He**

was   **elected**   **secretary**   **-**   **treasurer**

voted   writer-person,   money-keeper

R-on-L

of   **their**   **church.**   13. **John**   **is**

R-on-L   R-in-L   R-on-L   WA

   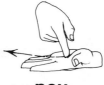

principal   **of**   **that**   **school.**   14. **The***

government   **requires**   **us**   **to***   **pay**

capitol   requests
             demands

                                  WA

taxes.   15. **Did**   **you**   **see**   **the***   **King**

cost   "K".

charge

* OPTIONAL

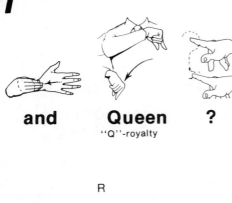

and　　**Queen**　　**?**
"Q"-royalty

WA

16. **The**[*]　　**prince**
"P" royalty

R

was　　**not**　　**with**　　**them.**　　17. **He**　　**is**

WA　　BHA
　　　　2X

an　　**officer**　　**in**　　**the**[*]　　**Russian**　　**army.**
　　　　　　　　　　　　　　　　　　Communist　　strike twice

BHA
AA　　　　　　　　　　WA

18. **He**　　**served**　　**during**　　**the**[*]　　**Korean**　　**War.**
　　　　serving tray　　while　　　　　　　　　　battle

WA　　　　　　　RL　　　WA

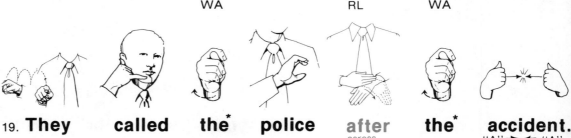

19. **They**　　**called**　　**the**[*]　　**police**　　**after**　　**the**[*]　　**accident.**
　　　　　　　　　　　　"C"　　across　　　　　"A" ➤ ◄ "A"
　　　　　　　　　　　or star

[*]
OPTIONAL

152

WA

20. **A**   **nurse**   came   **with**   **the***   **doctor.**

"N" at pulse   come   "D" or "M" at pulse

WORD	SYNONYM	MEMORY AID	SENTENCE
along	—	—	1
clothes	—	—	8
doctor	—	"D" or "M" at pulse	20
dull	—	—	9
elected	voted	—	12
famous	—	small announcement	6
garden	—	hoeing	2
government	capitol	—	14
grass	—	grow + green	2
King	—	"K" - royalty	15
knife	—	—	9
Korean	—	—	18
nurse	—	"N" at pulse	20
officer	—	—	17
perfect	—	"P"	7
police	—	"C" or "5" claw hand	19
prince	—	"P" - royalty	16
principal	—	—	13
profit	—	money in watch pockets	3

WORD	SYNONYM	MEMORY AID	SENTENCE
Queen	—	"Q" - royalty	15
Russian	communist	—	17
sea	—	W + waves ➤R	1
secretary-treasurer	—	writer-person, money-keeper	12
sharp	—	—	9
shore	—	tip of R hand to tip of L twice	1
smooth	—	—	8
subtracted	take away	—	3
sweetheart	—	—	11
take care of	—	keep C-C-W	2
taxes	cost	—	14
thin	—	thin cheeks	5
war	battle	—	18

*

OPTIONAL

WA

1. **The***   **person**   **who**   **doesn't**   **pay**   **tithes**

"P"s

don't
not

WA

1/10

is   **a**   **thief.**

robber
mask on face

2. **Jesus**   **called**

named

BHA   R-on-L

the*   **Pharisees**   **"hypocrites."**   3. **We**

"P"s in square on chest

F►R

lived   **in**   **a**   **tent**   **during**   **camp**

"V"s

while

two
tents

F►R   WF

meeting.   4. **She**   **put**   **candles**

service

placed

* OPTIONAL

WA

on   **the***   **cake.**
hot cross buns

5. **Did**   **you**

R➤L   R-on-L

bring   **your**   **umbrella**   **?**

6. **Did**

R-on-L   R-in-L
              2X

you   **wash**   **with**   **soap**   **?**
      "A" hands

7. **I**

           R-in-L   2X

need   **a**   **knife,**   **fork**   **and**   **spoon.**
must   R "V"
should
ought
ought to
etc.

               R

8. **He**   **forgot**   **his**   **toothbrush.**
     wiped off mind

9. **Paul**

***** OPTIONAL

R-U-L   CW

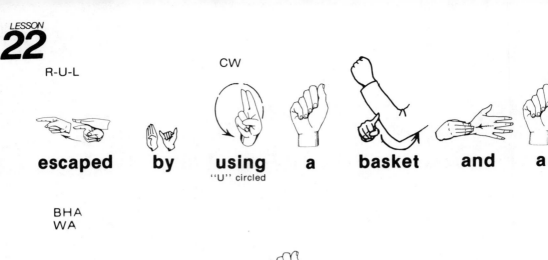

escaped   **by**   **using**   **a**   **basket**   **and**   **a**

"U" circled

BHA
WA

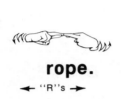

rope.

← "R"s →

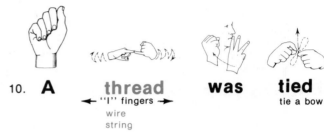

10. **A**   **thread**   **was**   **tied**

← "I" fingers →
wire
string

tie a bow

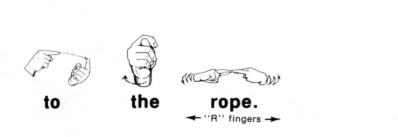

to   **the**   **rope.**

← "R" fingers →

11. **He**   **lost**

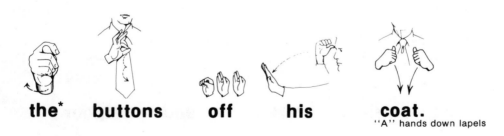

the*   **buttons**   **off**   **his**   **coat.**

"A" hands down lapels

R-in-L

12. **We**   **lost**   **the***   **game.**

challenge

13. **I**

*OPTIONAL

C-C-W

heard **the*** **wedding** **was** **beautiful.**
"C" at R ear   R hand in L   pretty
lovely

14. **He** **gave** **her** **a** **diamond** **as**
"D" at ring finger

an **engagement** **ring.** 15. **I** **had**
"E" at L ring finger

R-on-L

another **engagement (appointment)** **so** **I** **could**
other   can
able

R   → R

not **go.** 16. **He** **has** **a**

*
OPTIONAL

157

nice   **personality**   **and**   **a**   **fine**   **character.**

clean   "P" over L chest circled   "5"hand   "C" like personality

       C—C—W

17. **My**   **glasses**   **cost**   **two dollars**   **and**   **10 cents.**

                                             penny ten

                                      R-in-L   R-in-L

   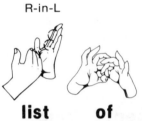

18. **Please**   **take**   **this**   **list**   **of**   **rules**   **with**

enjoy   "R"

pleasure

                                 WA

you.   19. **The**   **foundation**   **of**   **the**

                         support to L arm

                         R-in-L

building   **is**   **very**   **weak.**   20. **The**

house   "V"s

* OPTIONAL

R-on-L   R-in-L

hospital   is   an   institution   of   medicine.
cross on L shoulder   "I"

WORD	SYNONYM	MEMORY AID	SENTENCE
another	other	—	15
basket	—	—	9
building	house	—	19
buttons	—	—	11
camp	—	2 tents	3
candles	—	—	4
10 cents	—	penny ten	17
character	—	"C" like personality	16
cost	—	—	17
diamond	—	—	14
dollars	—	—	17
engagement	—	"E" at L ring finger	14
engagement (time for appointment)	—	—	15
fork	—	—	7
foundation	—	support to L arm	19
glasses (eye)	—	—	17

WORD	SYNONYM	MEMORY AID	SENTENCE
hospital	—	cross on L shoulder	20
hypocrites	—	—	2
institution	—	"I"	20
list	—	—	18
lost (lose)	—	—	11
medicine	—	—	20
personality	—	"P" over L chest circled C-C-W	16
Pharisees	—	"P" in square on chest	2
ring	—	—	14
rope	—	"R"	9
soap	—	—	6
spoon	—	—	7
tent	—	"V"s	3
thief	robber	mask on face	1
thread	—	"I" fingers	10
tied (a knot)	—	—	10
tithes	—	"1/10"	1
toothbrush	—	—	8
umbrella	—	—	5
wedding	—	R hand in L	13

WA

WA

1. **He**   **was**   **permitted**   **to***   **leave**   **the***

"let" with "P"s

R-on-L

WA   F→L

   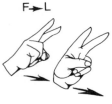

jail   **for**   **the***   **funeral.**   2. **He**

bars with
"four" hands

"V"s behind each
other = pallbearers

OUT
AA
WA   R-in-L   BHA   R-U-L

  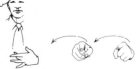

became   **sick**   **as**   **the***   **ship**   **went**   **under**

head-stomach

WA

RL

the*   **bridge.**   3. **After**   **arriving**   **at**

"V" supports like
foundation

across

BHA
OUT
WA   AA

the*   **island**   **they**   **went**   **horseback riding.**

"I"

* OPTIONAL

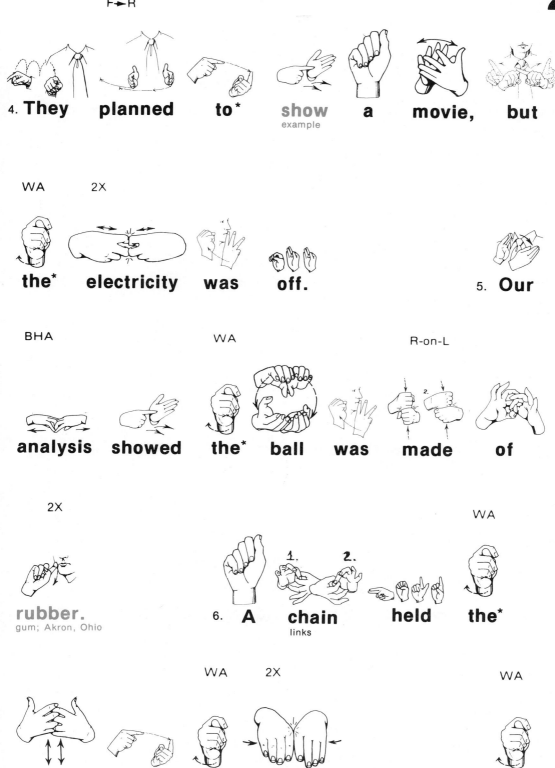

F ► R

4. **They** **planned** **to** * **show** a **movie,** **but**
example

WA   2X

the * **electricity** **was** **off.** 5. **Our**

BHA   WA   R-on-L

analysis **showed** **the** * **ball** **was** **made** **of**

2X

rubber. 6. **A** **chain** **held** **the** *
gum; Akron, Ohio   links

WA   WA   2X   WA

machine **to** **the** * **floor.** 7. **The** *
motor   "B" hands

* OPTIONAL

R-on-L

table   **was**   **made**   **of**   **wood,**   **but**   **had**

legs + top   sawing wood

great   **value.**   8. **He**   **was**   **responsible**

        "V" like special   "R"'s to R
                                                      shoulder

WA

for   **the***   **poem**   **which**   **was**   **read.**

                 "P" + song   that

WA   R-in-L   ➤ R   R-in-L

9. **The***   **new**   **equipment**   **developed**   **his**   **energy.**

                       "E" + thing   "D"   "E" + strong

                                                  R- ⋀ on-L
                                                  2X

WA

10. **The***   **normal**   **[abnormal]**   **person**   **will**   **function**

            "N"   "P"'s   "F"

* OPTIONAL

maturely.

"M" + full

11. **My** **reaction** **was** **that**

"R" "R"

WA   R-on-L

R-on-L

the* **metal** **was** **reliable.** 12. **The***

"M" "R"'s

R   R

evolution **theory** **changed** **his** **attitude.**

"E" + change   "T" + reason   "A" over heart, circled

13. **The*** **effect** **of** **the*** **psychiatrist** **in** **the***

"E"   "P" at pulse

BHA
AA   R-on-L

play **spoiled** **it.** 14. **The*** **psychology**

act
drama   "Ψ"

* OPTIONAL

AA
BHA

WA

workshop
"W" "S"

created
invent + made

dialogue.
"D" + talk

15. **The***

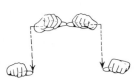

architecture
"A"'s

was

a

symbol
"S" + show

of

Egypt.
"X" on forehead

R-in-L

16. **They**

repeated
"R" + again

the*

story

although
doesn't
matter, never-the-less

it

R

R-on-L

 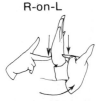

was

fiction.
"F" + imaginary

17. **The***

program
"P"

R-in-L
WA

emphasized
impress

a

progressive
"P" + improve

social
"S" + class

population.
"5" + "P"
L   R

* OPTIONAL

164

WA   R-on-L   R-in-L

18. **The** *   **result**   **was**   **the** *   **team**   **lost**   **the** *   game.
        "R" +   "T" +   R   challenge
        complete   class   "V"

  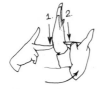 

19. **The** *   **program**   **represented**   **India**   **well.**
                            "R" + show

                                                    2X

20. **Idioms**   **are**   **a**   **universal**   **response**   **to**   **the** *
    "I" + " "   "U" +   "R" + answer
                                   world

environment.
"E"

WORD	SYNONYM	MEMORY AID	SENTENCE
although	doesn't matter, nevertheless	—	16
analysis	—	—	5
architecture	—	"A"s	15
attitude	—	"A" over heart circled	12
ball	—	—	5
bridge	—	"V" supports like foundation	2
chain	—	links	6
created	—	invent + made	14
developed	—	"D"	9
dialogue	—	"D" + talk	14
effect	—	"E"	13
Egypt	—	"X" on forehead	15
electricity	—	—	4
emphasis	impress	—	17
energy	—	"E" + strong	9
environment	—	"E"	20
equipment	—	"E" + thing	9
evolution	—	"E" + change	12
fiction	—	"F" + imagintion	16
floor	—	"B" hands	6
function	—	"F"	10
funeral	—	"V" behind each other = pallbearers	1
great	—	—	7
horseback riding	—	—	3
idioms	—	"I" + " "	20
India	—	—	19
island	—	"I"	3

WORD	SYNONYM	MEMORY AID	SENTENCE
jail	—	bars with "4" hands	1
machine	motor	—	6
maturely	—	"M" + full	10
metal	—	"M"	11
normal	—	"N"	10
permitted	—	"let with "P"s	1
play (drama)	act	—	13
poem	—	"P" + song	8
population	—	"5" + "P"	17
progressive	—	"P" + improve	17
psychiatrist	—	"P" at pulse	13
psychology	—	"P"	14
reaction	—	"R"."R"	11
reliable	—	"R"s	11
repeated	—	"R" + again	16
represented	—	"R" + show	19
response	—	"R" + answer	20
responsible	—	"R"s to R shoulder	8
result	—	"R" + complete	18
rubber	gum, Akron, Ohio	—	5
ship	—	—	2
social	—	"S" + class	17
symbol	—	"S" + show	15
team	—	"T" + class	18
theory	—	"T" + reason	12
under	—	—	2
universal	—	"U" + world	20
value	—	"V" like special	7
wood	—	sawing wood	7
workshop	—	"W"."S"	14

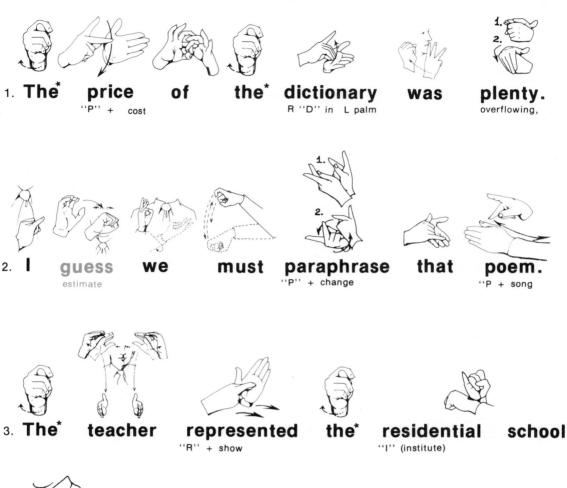

1. **The** **price** **of** **the** **dictionary** **was** **plenty.**
   "P" + cost   R "D" in L palm   overflowing,

2. **I** **guess** **we** **must** **paraphrase** **that** **poem.**
   estimate   "P" + change   "P + song

3. **The** **teacher** **represented** **the** **residential** **school**
   "R" + show   "I" (institute)

authority.
"A" + strong

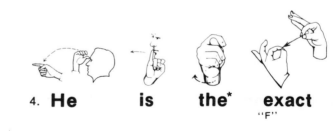

4. **He** **is** **the** **exact**
   "F"

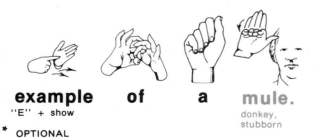

example **of** **a** **mule.**
"E" + show   donkey,
stubborn

5. **I** **admit**
   confess

* OPTIONAL

WA

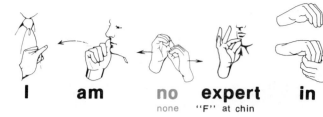

I   **am**   **no**   **expert**   **in**   **Algebra.**
          none   "F" at chin   "A"s + arithmetic

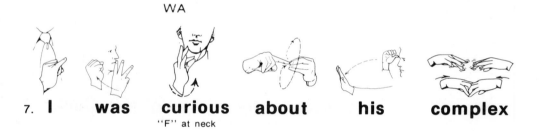

6. **I**   **wish**   **to**   **substitute**   **another**   **course.**
        want,   exchange, instead of   other   subject, lesson, sermon
        desire

WA

7. **I**   **was**   **curious**   **about**   **his**   **complex**
                        "F" at neck

WA

   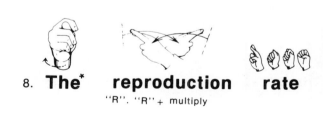

background.   8. **The***   **reproduction**   **rate**
                                 "R". "R" + multiply

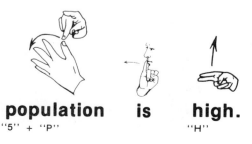

of   **the***   **population**   **is**   **high.**   9. **Organs**
                    "5" + "P"   "H"   "O" "O"

* OPTIONAL

168

WA

in **the*** **body** **do** **not** **regenerate** **themselves.**

"R" + again + grow

AA

10. **We** **will** **evaluate** **our** registration techniques.

"E"s + judge / register / skills, experience

11. **It** **is** **all right** **to*** **demonstrate** **emotion.**

"D" + show / "E" + feel

12. **I** asked **him** **to*** abbreviate **his** **report.**

requested prayed / condense / "R" at L wrist

2X   2X

13. **The*** **Coke** **advertisement** **illustration** **was** **cute.**

R at L arm / "I" + show / "H" on chin

* OPTIONAL

169

WA   AA

14. **The***   **drama**   **was**   **a**   **boring**   **disappointment.**
      act, play   dry under   miss as miss someone who is gone
                               chin

2X

15. **Congratulations**   **on**   **cancelling**   **that**   **correspondence**
     praise   correcting
     clap hands   criticize

     course.   16. **He**   **applied**   **the***   **copy**
     subject,
     lesson

   of   **the***   **picture**   **to**   **the***   **door.**

BHA
AA

17. **He**   **cannot**   **communicate**   **well.**
      R forefinger
      hits left forefinger

* OPTIONAL

18. **She** **only** **added** **to** **his** **disappointment.**
    alone   R on chin

WA

19. **The**[*] **sugar** **dissolved** **in** **the**[*] **tea.**
    sweet   "D" + disappeared   twist R in L
    Down mouth

2X   AA

20. **They** **functioned** **like** **professional** **people** **and**
    "F" + work   "P" + straight   "P"'s

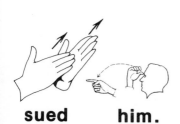

sued **him.**

WORD	SYNONYM	MEMORY AID	SENTENCE
abbreviate	condense	—	12
added	—	—	18
admit	confess	—	5
advertisement	—	—	13
algebra	—	"A" + arith-metic	5
all right	—	—	11
applied	—	—	16
authority	—	"A" + strong	3
background	—	—	7
body	—	—	9
boring	—	dry under chin	14
cancelling	correcting, criticize	—	15
coke	—	R at L arm	13
communicate	—	—	17
complex	—	—	7
congratula-tions	praise	—	15
copy	—	—	16
correspond-ence	—	—	15
course	subject, lesson sermon	—	6,
curious	—	"F" at neck	7
cute	—	"H" on chin	13
demonstrate	—	"D" + show	11

WORD	SYNONYM	MEMORY AID	SENTENCE
dictionary	—	R "D" in L palm	1
disappoint-ment	bitter, miss	R on chin	14,
dissolved	—	"D" + dis-appeared	19
drama	act, play,	—	14
emotion	—	"E" ÷ feel	11
evaluate	—	"E"'s + judge	10
exact	—	"F"	4
expert	—	"F" at chin	5
illustration	—	"I" + show	13
organs	—	"O" "O"	9
paraphrase	—	"P" + change	2
plenty	enough	overflowing	1
price	—	"P" + cost	1
professional	—	"P" + straight	20
regenerate	—	"R" + again + grow	9
registration	register	—	10
report	—	"R" at wrist	12
reproduction	—	"R","R" + multiply	8
residential	—	"I" (institute)	3
school			
substitute	exchange, instead	—	6
sued	—	—	20
techiques	skills, experi-ence	—	10

WA

R-U-L
→ R

1. **The***   **frightened**   **pigs**   **ran**   **into**   **the***   **sea.**

R under chin

"W" at mouth + waves → R

2. **The***   **butterfly**   **cannot**   **fly**   **as**   **high**

hooked thumbs

"H"

as   **the***   **eagle.**   3. **The***   **bear**

forefinger hooks nose

crossed arms crook fingers

2X

is   **a**   **slow**   **moving**   **animal.**

"AND" hands to the right

4. **During**   **the***   **Millenium**   **the***   **lion**   **and**

While

1000 years

mane over head

* OPTIONAL

173

WA

WA

the*   **wolf**   **shall**   **play**   **together.**
nose   with and
                                            circle CCW

5. **Africa**   **is**   **well**   **known**   **for**   **its**
"A"   know
                             knowledge

monkeys.   6. **She**   **hates**   **worms,**   **bees,**
scratch   snap center   wiggle across   "F" at
                         fingers out   L hand   cheek

flies,   **and**   **spiders.**   7. **He**   **likes**
catching   hook little fingers and crawl   prefers,
on arm

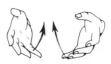   

basketball,   **volleyball,**   **wrestling,**   **and**   **swimming.**
pantomime   pantomime   pantomime

*OPTIONAL

174

WA

8. **His**	**friend**	**would**	**rather**	**play**	**tennis.**
	hook forefingers	"WD"	better	"Y"	

WA

9. **The**	**national**	**game**	**of**	**baseball**	**is**	**my**
	nation	challenge		pantomime		

favorite.
pet

10. **We**   **are**   **planning**   **a**

BHA
OUT
AA

"P"."P" → R

trip	**to**	**visit**	**the**	**country**	**of**
		"V"s		"Y" at L elbow and circle C-C-W	

BHA
OUT
AA

Sweden.	11. **Last**	**year**	**we**	**visited**
"S" at forehead	past			"V"s

* OPTIONAL

Norway,
"N" at
forehead
circle
C-C-W

Denmark,
"D" at fore-
head, circle
C-C-W

and

Finland.
"F" at forehead
circle C-C-W

WA

12. **He**

came

to

theˑ

U.S.
circle
CW

from

WA

China.
forefinger at R eye

13. **He**

is

an

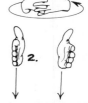

American

Indian.
war paint

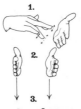

14. **One**

student
study person

came

from

AA

Malaysia
for dance

and

two

from

Jamaica.
island

* OPTIONAL

BHA
AA
IN

15. **In**   **Mexico**   **the**   **people**   **speak**   **Spanish.**
"M" on R
cheek   "P"s   say, tell

16. **He**   **likes**   **ping-pong,**   **but**   **loses**   **at**
prefers   pantomime   "V"

bowling.   17. **Snakes**   **are**   **dangerous**
pantomime   for fangs   danger

2X

pets.   18. **Rabbits**   **are**   **very**   **fast.**
"H"s   "V"s   quick
crossed
wrists

19. **My**   **father**   **has**   **several**   **horses.**
few

177

20. **The** **children** **love** **animals.**

crossed arms
on chest

WORD	SYNONYM	MEMORY AID	SENTENCE	WORD	SYNONYM	MEMORY AID	SENTENCE
baseball	—	pantomime	9	Malaysia	—	for dance	14
basketball	—	pantomime	7	Mexico	—	"M" on R cheek	15
bear	—	crossed arms	3				
bees	—	"F" at cheek	6	millenium	—	1000 years	4
bowling	—	pantomime	16	monkeys	—	scratch	5
butterfly	—	hooked thumbs	2	national	nation	—	9
China	—	forefinger at R eye	12	Norway	—	"N" at forehead	11
country	—	"Y" at L elbow and circle C-C-W	10	pigs	—	R under chin	1
				ping-pong	—	pantomime	16
				rabbits	—	"H"'s crossed wrists	18
dangerous	danger	—	17				
Denmark	—	"D" at forehead	11	several	few	—	19
				snakes	—	for fangs	17
eagle	—	forefinger hooks nose	2	spiders	—	hook little fingers and crawl	6
favorite	pet	—	9	Sweden	—	"S" at forehead	10
Finland	—	"F" at forehead, circle C-C-W	11				
				swimming	—	pantomime	7
flies	—	catching on arm	6	tennis	—	—	8
				U. S.	—	circle CW	12
frightened	—	—	1	volleyball	—	pantomime	7
Indian	—	war paint	13	wolf	—	nose	4
Jamaica	—	island	14	worms	—	—	6
lion	—	mane over head	4	wrestling	—	—	7

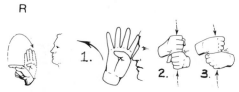

1. **God** **created**
invent + made
the * **heavens** **and** **the** *

earth. 2. **Adam**
"A"
and **Eve**
"E"
were

created **last.** 3. **The** * **covenant**
invent + made | finally | agree + "C" as "same"

God **made** **with** **Abraham** **required** **a**
"A" at L elbow | demand request

blood **sacrifice.** 4. **David** **was**
red + flow over L hand | "S" + offer | "D"

* OPTIONAL

R-on-L

F➤L

accused
blamed,
at fault

of

adultery.
L"V"-R "A"

5. **Disciples**
"D" + follow

WA

make

atonement

at

the*

altar
"A" "A"

R-U-L

R-in-L

R-in-L

6. **Paul's**

epistles
letter

emphasize
impress

conversion

and

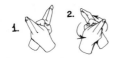

repentance.
"R" + change

7. **The***

fruit
"F" at chin

of

the*

2X

R-in-L

Spirit
ghost

is

love,

joy
happiness

and

peace.

* OPTIONAL

8. **Wicked**
w + bad

men

crucified
nail -hammer, then R
and outstretched arms

Jesus
nail prints

at

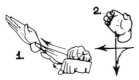

Calvary.
rock + mountain + cross

WA   2X   R-in-L

9. **The** *

gospel
''G'' in L hand

emphasizes
impress

R-in-L

that

Jesus
nail prints

is

Messiah.
''M'' + royalty sign

10. **Moses**

BHA
AA
IN

celebrated
anniversary

Passover

with

his

people.
''P''s

BHA
AA

11. **The** *

Jewish
goatee

rabbi

was

in charge of
controls,
reigns,rules

the *

* OPTIONAL

temple.
"T" + church

WA

12. **The***

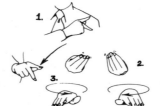

kingdom
king + land, soil

of

R

God

is

no
none

myth.

R

13. **His**

WA

testimony
lecture, speech

of

the*

miracle
wonderful + work

was

a

blessing.

14. **I**

EA
2X

preach
"F" + lecture

nothing
none + open "5" hands

except
L lifts R

Jesus
nail prints

R

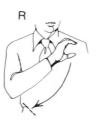

Christ.
"C" + royalty

15. **My**

* OPTIONAL

R

religion
"R" at heart,
down and out

believes
trusts
mind grasps

in

divine
"D" + clean

healing
whole,
well,
health

by

faith.
mind grasps

16. **Christians**
Jesus + person,
Christ + person

who
whom

backslide
R "A" backs away
from L "A"

WA

lose

R-in-L

their

crown.
R&L thumb and center fingers
grasp crown and put on head
R-in-L

17. **The**

priest
on chest

L ⌐_____⌐ R

in

the*

Old
age

Testament
"T" + law

understood
light goes on

the*

Trinity.
3 in 1

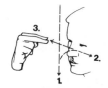
18. **Many**

R

Catholic
sign of cross in front
of face

R

priests
collar

* OPTIONAL

183

R

are

missionaries.
R "M" circled at L shoulder

19. **Isaiah**  **was**

R-U-L

a

1. 2.

prophet
see + look + person

with

a

R-U-L

vision.
R see under L hand

20. **Blessed**
"A"s

WA

are

the*

1. 2.

pure
"P" + clean

in

heart
draw heart on
L chest

and

mind.
forefinger to
forehead

WORD	SYNONYM	MEMORY AID	SENTENCE
Abraham	—	"A"s like father or R "A" at L elbow	3
Adam	—	"A"	2
adultery	—	L "V" - R "A"	4
altar	—	"A""A"	5
backslide	—	R"A" backs away from	16
blessing	—	—	13
blood	—	red + flow over L hand	3
Calvary	—	rock + mountain + cross	8

WORD	SYNONYM	MEMORY AID	SENTENCE
celebrated	anniversary	—	10
Christ	—	"C" + royalty	14
Christians	—	Jesus + person Christ + person	16
covenant	—	agree + "C" (same as)	3
crown	—	R & L thumb and center fingers grasp crown and put on head	16
crucified	—	nail-hammer, then R and outstretched arms	8

*
OPTIONAL

WORD	SYNONYM	MEMORY AID	SENTENCE
David	—	"D" like king	4
disciples	—	"D" + follow	5
divine	—	"D" + clean	15
earth	—	—	1
epistles	—	"E" + letter	6
Eve	—	"E"	2
except	—	L lifts R	14
faith	—	mind grasps	15
fruit	—	"F" at chin	7
gospel	—	"G" in L hand	9
healing	—	whole, well, health	15
heart	—	draw heart on L chest	20
heavens	—	—	1
in charge of	controls, rules reigns	—	11
kingdom	—	king + soil, land	12
Messiah	—	M + royalty sign	9
mind	—	forefinger to forehead	20
miracle	—	—	13
myth	—	—	12

WORD	SYNONYM	MEMORY AID	SENTENCE
nothing	—	none + open "5" hands	14
old	age	—	17
Paul	—	"P"	6
peace	—	—	7
priest (O.T.)	—	on chest	17
priest (Catholic)	—	collar	19
prophet	—	see + look + person	19
pure	—	"P" + clean	20
rabbi	—	"R"."R" down chest	11
religion	—	"R" at heart out and up	15
repentance	—	"R" + change	6
sacrifice	—	"S" + offer	3
spirit	ghost	—	7
temple	—	"T" + church	11
testament	—	"T" + law	17
testimony	lecture, speech	—	13
trinity	—	3 in 1	17
vision	—	R see under L hand	19
wicked	—	"w" + bad	8

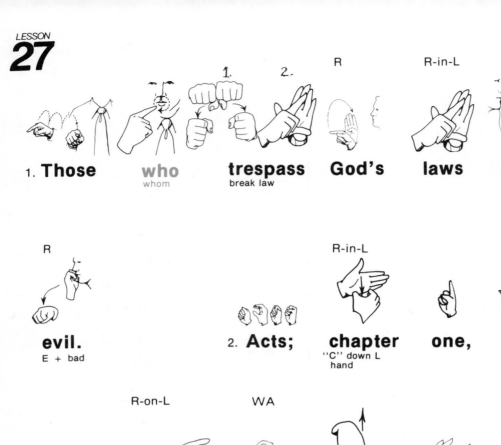

1. **Those** — who (*whom*) — **trespass** (*break law*) — **God's** — **laws** — **are**

evil. (*E + bad*)

2. **Acts;** — **chapter** (*"C" down L hand*) — **one,** — **verse** (*L → R across L palm*)

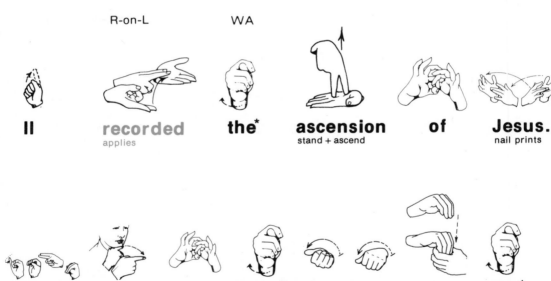

II — recorded (*applies*) — **the*** — **ascension** (*stand + ascend*) — **of** — **Jesus.** (*nail prints*)

3. **John** — **spoke** (*say, tell speak*) — **of** — **the*** — **baptism** (*"A" "A" → R*) — **in** — **the***

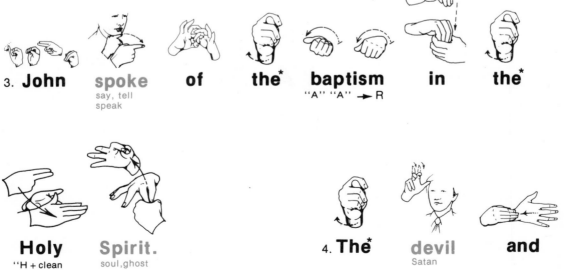

Holy (*"H + clean*) — **Spirit.** (*soul, ghost*)

4. **The*** — devil (*Satan*) — **and**

* OPTIONAL

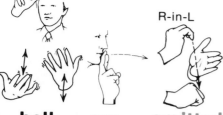

R-in-L

2X

hell
devil + fire

are

omitted
subtracted

from

sermons
lessons,
messages

preached
"F" + lecture

C-C-W

today.
now day

5. **Do** **you** **think** **angels**
both hands

R

R-O-L

have **wings** **?**
1 hand

6. **Anointing** **with**
"A"

R-U-L

WA

oil **and** **praying** **for** **the*** **sick** **is**
ask   head,
                   stomach

R►L

scriptural.
verse, Biblical

7. **The*** **Bible** **warns** **against**
        Jesus book   R hits L

*
OPTIONAL

187

WA

worshiping
adore, amen

images
"A"

or

idols.
"I"

8. **The***

BHA
AA
IN

WA

people
"P"'s

broke

the*

Ten
(10)

Commandments.
"C" + law

R

R

R

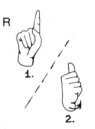

9. **He**

was

convicted
heart jabbed

because

he

did not

R-in-L

R

BHA
AA
OUT

1.

2.

pay

tithes.
1/10th

10. **We**

went

to

R-in-L

R-on-L

WA

the*

Presbyterian
"P"

church
"C"

at

Christmas
"C"

and

*
OPTIONAL

WA

Easter.
"E" "E"

WA

11. **The** **Mennonite** **lady** **had**
prayer bonnet ties   woman +
                       "ruffles"

R-in-L

a **Lutheran** **husband.**   12. **The**
"L"   man + marry

R-in-L   R-on-L

protestant **group** **promised** **to** **deliver** **him.**
kneeling   "G" + class   "D" like save

R-in-L   R-in-L

13. **The** **parables** **illustrate** **divine** **truth.**
"P"   "I" + show   "D" + clean   honest, true
                                       "H"

WA

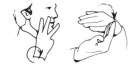

14. **Communion** **was** **instituted** **by** **Jesus**
wine + bread   started,   nail prints
                      begun

OPTIONAL

R   R

15. **Jesus**
nail prints

said,
say, tell,
speak

"Not

my

will,
"W" + law

but

thine
possessive

be

done."

16. **Jesus**
Nail prints

delivers
"D" + save

from

temptations
R➤L elbow

and

demons.
Satan + spirits

W A   R   R-on-L

17. **The***

Lord
"L" + royalty

is

my

shepherd
sheep + keeper

and

the

Lamb
sheep + small

of

God.

18. **He**

* OPTIONAL

WA

leads
L pulls
R→L

me

beside
next

the[*]

still
quiet

R
WF

waters.
"W" + flow → R

19. **Thy**
poss.

rod

and

thy

R→F
R

staff,
holding staff

they

comfort
R—on—L,
cupped hand

me.

20. **Thou**

preparest
"P" "P"

a

table
legs + top

before
in front of,
presence of

me

and

mercy
pity
feel + sympathy

shall

follow
R follows L

me.

* OPTIONAL

191

WORD	SYNONYM	MEMORY AID	SENTENCE	WORD	SYNONYM	MEMORY AID	SENTENCE
angels	—	both hands	5	Mennonite	—	prayer bonnet ties	11
anointing	—	"A"	6	mercy	—	feel + sympathy	20
ascension	—	stand + ascend	2	oil	—	—	6
baptism	—	"A" "A"➤R	3	omitted	subtracted	—	4
beside	next	—	18	parables	—	—	13
chapter	—	"C" down L hand	2	praying	ask	—	6
Christmas	—	"C"	10	Presbyterian	—	"P"	10
command-ments	—	"C" + law	8	Protestant	—	kneeling	12
communion	—	wine + bread	14	records	applies	—	2
convicted	—	heart jabbed	9	rod	—	—	19
demons	—	Satan + spirits	16	scriptural	verse	—	6
devil	satan	—	4	shepherd	—	sheep ÷ keeper	17
Easter	—	"E"."E'	10	staff	—	holding staff	19
evil	—	"E" + bad	1	still	—	—	18
hell	—	devil + fire	4	trespass	—	break + law	1
holy	—	"H" + clean	3	truth	honest, true	"H"	13
idols	—	"I"	7	verse	—	L➤R across L palm	2
illustrate	—	"I" + show	13	will	—	"W" + law	15
images	—	"A"	7	wings	—	1 hand	5
lamb	—	sheep + small	17	worshipping	adore, amen	—	7
Lord	—	"L" + loyalty	17				

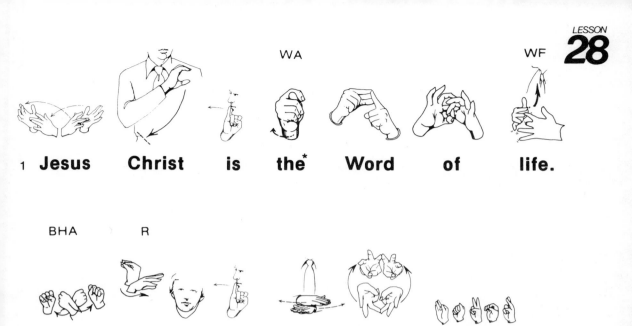

1. **Jesus**   **Christ**   WA **is**   **the**[*]   **Word**   **of**   WF **life.**

BHA   R

2. **Saving**
save, safe   **grace**   **is**   **unworthy**
not + "W" + important   **favor.**

R-in-L

3. **Glory,**
shake hand
as it rises   **hallelujah,**
clap + win   **I**   **am**   **on**   **my**

way
"W" + street   **to**   **heaven.**   4. **I**   **praise**
congratulations
clap hands   **God**

R-on-L

who   **redeemed**
"R" + save   **us**   **from**   **the**[*]   **earth.**

[*]OPTIONAL

193

WA

5. **Jesus** **did not** **condemn**
accuse,
blame
the* **world.**
"W" + year

2X

6. **The*** **Jews** **passed** **through** **the** **wilderness**
dry + land

BHA
AA
IN

AA
IN

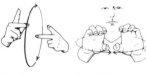

7. **The*** **long** **revival** **made** **the*** **congregation**
thrill, excite
people + class

R-in-L

weary.
tired

8. **Jesus** **paid** **the*** **supreme**
"A" up

price
cost
*
OPTIONAL

for **victory.**
"V" hands

9. **It** **will**

   2X R-on-L

be   **a**   **thrilling,**   **wonderful**   **time**   **in**   **heaven.**

enthrall, excited,
revival

R-in-L

10. **We**   **can**   **say**   **"amen"**   **to**   **his**

R-on-L   R-in-L

    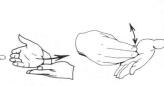

ministry.   11. **We**   **take**   **this**   **offering**

"M" + work   gather + money

for   **world**   **missions.**   12. **Decisions**

"W" + year   missionary

CW

for   **Christ**   **are**   **for**   **time**   **and**   **eternity.**

eternal

BHA
IN
AA

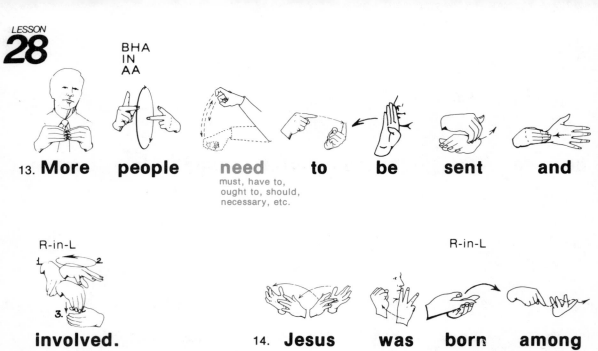

13. **More**   **people**   **need**   **to**   **be**   **sent**   **and**

must, have to,
ought to, should,
necessary, etc.

R-in-L

involved.

R-in-L

14. **Jesus**   **was**   **born**   **among**

WA

F ► R

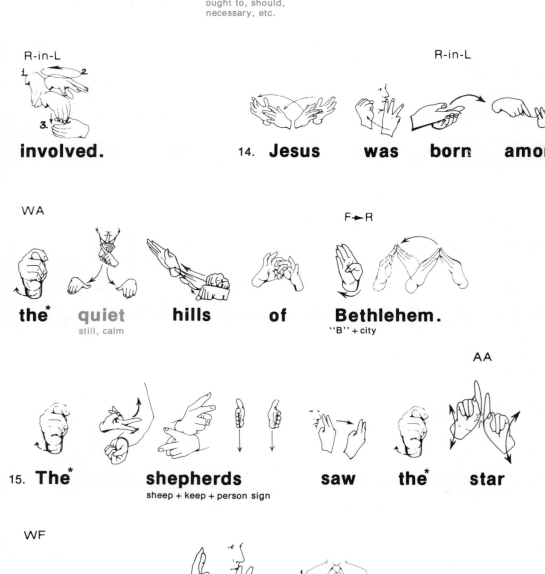

the *   **quiet**   **hills**   **of**   **Bethlehem.**

still, calm   "B" + city

AA

15. **The** *   **shepherds**   **saw**   **the** *   **star**

sheep + keep + person sign

WF

shining   **and**   **were**   **fearful.**   16. **The** *

afraid, frightened

*
OPTIONAL

R-on-L   WA

Angels   **made**   **the***   **announcement**   **of**   **baby**

announces

R-on-L   2X

Jesus'   **birth.**   17. **The***   **faithful**   **Wise**

"F" hands

R►B   F►L

Men   **brought**   **gifts**   **to**   **the***   **sleeping**

Christ.   18. **Jesus**   **is**   **Immanuel,**

God with us

CW

Counsellor,   **the***   **everlasting**   **Father.**

advisor   always, still, forever,
                                   eternity

*****
OPTIONAL

R-on-L

19. **Jesus**   **ministered**   **in**   **Judah,**   **but**   **was**

           "M" + work   Jews

R-on-L   R-in-L

rejected .   20. **The***   **risen**   **Christ**   **shall**

                           get up

                                  R   R-on-L

                                WA

descend   **with**   **power**   **the***   **second**   **time.**

come down   might, strong

WORD	SYNONYM	MEMORY AID	SENTENCE	WORD	SYNONYM	MEMORY AID	SENTENCE
amen	—	—	10	fearful	afraid, frightened	—	15
announcment	announces	—	16	gifts	—	—	17
baby	—	—	16	glory	—	—	3
Bethlehem	—	"B" + city	14	grace	—	—	2
condemn	accuse, blame	—	5	hallelujah	—	clap + win	3
congregation	—	class + people	7	hills	—	—	14
counsellor	advisor	—	18	Immanuel	—	God with us	18
descend	—	come down	20	involved	—	—	13
eternity	eternal	—	12	Judah	Jews	—	19
everlasting	—	—	18	ministered	—	"M" + work	19
faithful	—	"F" hands	17	ministry	—	"M" + work	10
				missions	—	—	11

* OPTIONAL

WORD	SYNONYM	MEMORY AID	SENTENCE
offering	—	gather + money	11
power	might, strong	—	20
redeemed	—	"R" + save	4
rejected	—	—	19
revival	thrill, excited	—	7
risen	—	get up	20
second	—	—	20
sent	—	—	13
shining	—	—	15
sleeping	—	—	17

WORD	SYNONYM	MEMORY AID	SENTENCE
star	—	—	17
supreme	—	"A" + up	8
thrilling	enthrall, excited, revival	—	9
through	—	—	6
unworthy	—	not + "W" + important	2
victory	—	"V" hands	8
weary	tired	—	7
wilderness	—	dry + land	6
wonderful	—	—	9
world	—	"W" + year	5,11

R-on-L

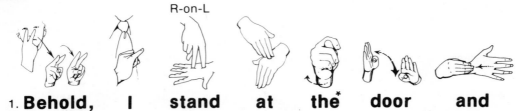

1. **Behold,**   **I**   **stand**   **at**   **the**   **door**   **and**

R-on-L   R-in-L

knock.   2. **Jesus**   **was**   **nailed**   **to**

nail + hit

the   **cross**   **for**   **our**   **sins.**   3. **Jesus**

L ↑↑ R

2X

knew   **sorrow**   **in**   **the**   **garden.**

knowledge   sorry   "A" over heart

4. **For**   **the**   **knowledge**   **of**   **the**   **Lord**   **shall**

know

* OPTIONAL

R-on-L · WA · R-on-L

fill **all** **the*** **earth.**

WF · R-on-L

5. **Rain** **fills**

WF · WF

the **rivers** **that** **flow** **into** **the*** **ocean.**
"W" + flow · → R · "W" + sea waves → R

6. **We** **shall** **praise** **and** adore **our** **dear**
clap · amen · "d" hands

Lord. 7. **The*** beauty **of** **the*** soul
"L" · beautiful, lovely, pretty · spirit, ghost

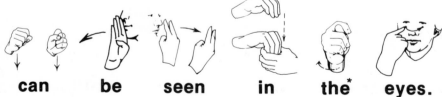

can **be** **seen** **in** **the*** **eyes.**

*
OPTIONAL

LESSON 29

2X

8. **I** **sing** **because** **I** **am** **happy** **I**
   song, music   glad, rejoice

heard **about** **Pentecost.**   9. **There** **is**

no **sin** **or** **shame** **in** **heaven,** **only**
none

L ↑ R

WA

righteousness.   10. **The*** **Christian**
Jesus + person

AA

walk **is** **narrow** **but** **rich** **and**
money + pile

* OPTIONAL

202

R

precious.

11. **My**

journey

shall

end

WA

at

the[*]

throne
chair + arms

in

the[*]

kingdom.
king + land

AA

WF

12. **This**

generation

might
possibly,
may be

be

alive
life

when

2X

R-on-L

the[*]

trumpet

calls.

13. **The**[*]

sun

R-O-L

and

moon

rise

over

the[*]

land.
soil + land

[*]
OPTIONAL

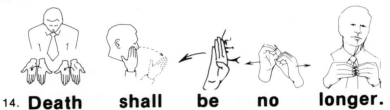

14. **Death**   **shall**   **be**   **no**   **longer.**   15. **The**[*]

dawning   **made**   **the**[*]   **shadow**   **of**   **the**[*]   **cross**

black + over

R-on-L

on   **the**[*]   **rock.**   16. **The**[*]   **noise**

	R-on-L	R-on-L	F►R

of   **conquered**   **nations**   **filled**   **Jerusalem.**

defeat, overcome   J + city

R-on-L

17. **The**[*]   **king**   **touched**   **the**[*]   **gold**   **crown**   **and**

ear + yellow

[*]
OPTIONAL

WA

smiled.
"5" hands

18.

He   took   a   second

bow   **after**   **they**   **were**   **gone.**

WA

  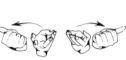  

19. **The***   **chains**   **disappeared**   **in**   **a**   **strange**
       links   vanished

way.   20. **Stephen**   **no**   **longer**   **felt**
                     more   feels

R-on-L   R-on-L

the*   **stones**   **upon**   **his**   **body.**

*
OPTIONAL

WORD	SYNONYM	MEMORY AID	SENTENCE
adore	amen	—	6
alive	life	—	12
beauty	beautiful,love-ly,pretty	—	7
behold	—	—	1
bow	—	—	18
conquered	defeat,over-come	—	16
dawning	—	—	15
dear	—	"D" + love	6
end	—	—	11
eyes	—	—	7
flow	—	➤R	5
generation	—	—	12
gold	—	ear + yellow	17
gone	—	—	18
Jerusalem	—	"J" + city	16
journey	—	—	11
knock	—	—	1
knowledge	know	—	4
land	—	soil + plain	13
might	possibly, maybe	—	12
moon	—	—	13
nailed	—	nailed + hit	2
narrow	—	—	10
nations	national	—	16
no	none	—	9
noise	—	—	16

WORD	SYNONYM	MEMORY AID	SENTENCE
no longer	—	—	14
ocean	sea	"W" + sea waves ➤R	5
Pentecost	—	—	8
praise	—	clap	6
precious	—	—	10
rain	—	—	5
rich	—	money	10
righteousness	—	—	9
rivers	—	"W" + flow ➤R	5
rock	—	—	15
seen	—	—	7
shadow	—	black + over	15
shall	—	—	6
shame	—	—	9
sins	—	—	2
sing	song, music	—	8
smiled	—	"5" hands	17
sorrow	sorry	"A" over heart	3
soul	spirit, ghost	—	7
stones	—	—	20
strange	—	—	19
sun	—	—	13
throne	—	chair + arms	11
trumpet	—	—	12
upon	—	—	20

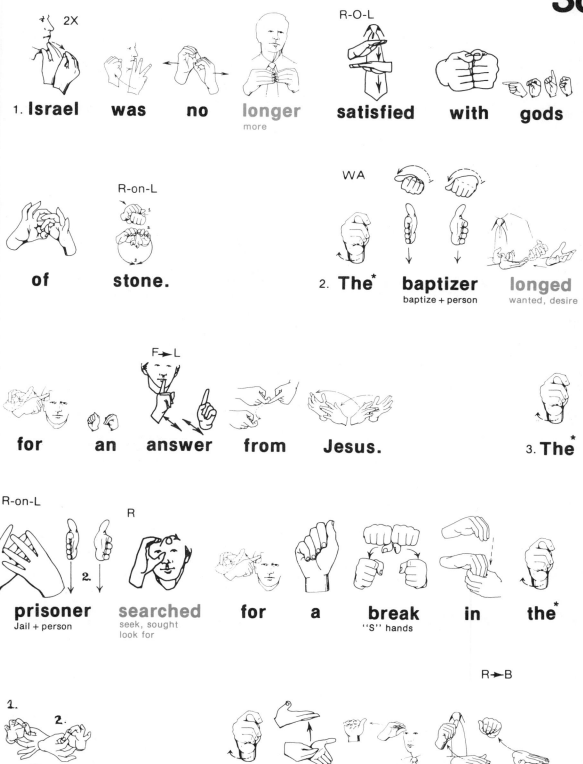

1. **Israel**   **was**   **no**   **longer**   **satisfied**   **with**   **gods**
more

of   **stone.**   2. **The***   **baptizer**   **longed**
baptize + person   wanted, desire

for   **an**   **answer**   **from**   **Jesus.**   3. **The***

prisoner   **searched**   **for**   **a**   **break**   **in**   **the***
Jail + person   seek, sought look for   "S" hands

chain.   4. **The***   **rich**   **man**   **left**
links   money + pile   depart leave

*
OPTIONAL

CW

without
with + drop

eternal
always, still
forever, everlasting

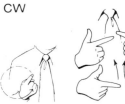

life.

WA

5. **The*** **woman**

2X

said
say, speak, tell

"yes",

to

the*

Saviour
save + person

at

the*

R-on-L

well.

6. **The***

great
big
large

Physician
"M" at pulse, doctor

made

2X

every

person
"P"'s + person

whole.
well, heal, healthy

7. **Therefore**
3 dots ∴

the*

WF

harvest

was

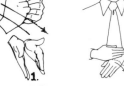
destroyed

after

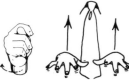
the* **flood.**
water rising

*
OPTIONAL

R-on-L

WA

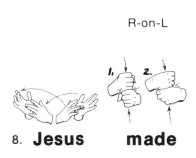    

8. **Jesus**   **made**   **more**   **wine**   **for**   **the***   **feast.**
banquet,
eating lots

2X   R-on-L

9. **Those**   **who**   **witness**   **must**   **keep**   **a**   cheery
smile

R-in-L   R-in-L

attitude.
"A" at heart

10. **One**   truly   **born**   **again**
verily

CW   CW

shall   **live**   **forever**   **and**   ever.
always

11. **Jesus'**   **mother,**   **Mary,**   **was**   **pregnant**   **by**   **the***
"5" hands

OPTIONAL

Holy
"H" + clean

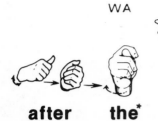

Spirit.
soul, ghost

AA

12. **We** **should** **walk**

WA

WA

after **the*** **Spirit** **not** **after** **the** **flesh.**
following   meat

R-on-L

13. **We** **owe** **God** **much** **for** **removing**

our **sin.** 14. **There** **was** **no** **place**
"P"   "P"

to* **bury** **Jesus.** 15. **The***
"A" + grave

*
OPTIONAL

210

2X

OUT

young
youth   **man**   **was**   **cross**
angry   **after**   **rolling**

WA

    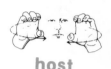

down   **the***   **hill.**   16. **The***   **host**
class

of   **angels**   **sang**
sing   **above.**
the sky   17. **Jesus**

2X

was   **asleep**
sleep   **on**   **that**   **kind**
"K" + world   **of**   **hay.**
claw hand
at mouth

18. **Then**   **we**   **shall**   **be**   **joined**
linked   **forever**

*
OPTIONAL

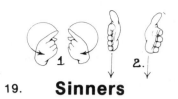

with **Him.** 19. **Sinners** **plunged**
dive, dove

WA   WF

  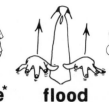

beneath **the*** **flood** **lose** **all** **their** **guilty**
under   water rising   convicting

R-in-L

stains. 20. **We** **are** **adopted** **into**
picked up,
assumed

the* **family** **of** **God.**
"F" + group

WORD	SYNONYM	MEMORY AID	SENTENCE	WORD	SYNONYM	MEMORY AID	SENTENCE
above	—	—	16	more	—	—	8
adopted	picked up, assumed	—	20	owe	—	—	13
				physician	doctor	"M" at pulse	6
answer	—	—	2	place	—	"P"."P"	14
asleep	sleep	—	17	plunged	dive, dove	—	19
beneath	under	—	19	pregnant	—	"5" hands	11
cheery	smile	—	9	prisoner	—	Jail + person	3
cross	angry	—	15	removing	—	—	13
eternal	forever, ever-lasting	always + still	4	rolling	—	—	15
				sang	sing	—	16
ever	always	—	10	satisfied	—	—	1
every	—	—	6	Saviour	—	save + person	5
feast	banquet	eating lots	8	searched	seek, sought, look for	—	3
flesh	meat	—	12				
flood	—	water rising	7	stains	—	—	19
guilty	—	convicting	19	therefore	—	—	7
harvest	—	—	7	truly	verily	—	10
hay	—	cupped hand at mouth	17	whole	well, heal, healthy	—	6
host	class	—	16	wine	—	—	8
Israel	Jews	—	1	without	—	with + drop	4
joined	linked	—	18	witness	—	—	9
kind	—	—	17	yes	—	—	5
longed	wanted, desired	—	2				

Appendixes

Choruses

to be sung in sign language

1. Amazing Grace

Amazing grace! How sweet
the sound,
That saved a wretch like me!
I once was lost, but now I'm
found,
Was blind, but now I see.

2. At The Cross

At the cross, at the cross,
where I first saw the light;
And the burden of my heart
rolled away;
It was there by faith, I
received my sight;
And now I am happy all
the day.

3. Christ Is The Answer*

Christ is the answer to all my
longing;
Christ is the answer to all my
need.
Savior, Baptizer, the great
Physician,
Oh, hallelujah! He's all
I need.

4. Cleanse Me

Oh, Holy Ghost, revival comes
from Thee.
Send a revival, start the work
in me.
Thy word declares, Thou wilt
supply our need
For blessings now, Oh, Lord
I humbly plead.

5. Come By Here, Lord*

Come by here, Lord, come by
here,
Come by here, Lord, come by
here;
Come by here, Lord, come by
here,
O Lord, come by here.

6. Everybody Ought To Know*

Everybody ought to know,
Everybody ought to know,
Everybody ought to know,
Who Jesus is.
He's the Lily of the Valley,
He's the bright and the
Morning Star,
He's the fairest of ten
thousand,
Everybody ought to know.

7. Fill Me Now

Fill me now, fill me now,
Jesus come and fill me now;
Fill me with Thy hallowed
presence
Come, O come and fill
me now.

8. Friendship With Jesus

Friendship with Jesus,
fellowship divine;
Oh what blessed sweet,
communion,
Jesus is a friend of mine.

9. Give Me Oil In My Lamp*

Give me oil in my lamp, keep
me burning,
Give me oil in my lamp
I pray;
Give me oil in my lamp, keep
me burning,
Keep me burning till the
break of day.
Sing, Sing, Sing, Sing;
Sing, hosanna, sing, hosanna,
Sing Hosanna to the King!

10. God Is Moving By His Spirit*

God is moving by His Spirit,
Moving thru all the earth;
Signs and wonders, when
God moveth.
Move, O Lord, in me.

11. Heavenly Sunshine*

Heavenly Sunshine, Heavenly
sunshine,
Flooding my soul with glory
divine;
Heavenly sunshine, heavenly
sunshine,
Hallelujah! Jesus is mine!

12. He's My King*

He's my King, and oh, I
dearly love Him,
He's my King, no other is
above him;
All day long, in raptured
praise I sing,
"Hallelujah, He's my King!"

13. He's The Lord Of Glory*

He's the Lord of Glory, He is
    the great I am;
He's the Alpha and the
    Omega, The beginning and
    the end.
His name is Wonderful, The
    Prince of Peace is He;
The Everlasting Father
    Throughout eternity.

14. He Was Nailed To The Cross

He was nailed to the cross for
    me,
He was nailed to the cross for
    me;
On the cross crucified, for me
    He died,
He was nailed to the cross for
    me.

15. Holy Is The Lord*

Holy is the Lord and mighty
    is His Name
King of heaven, yet down to
    earth He came;
Angels sing His praise, all
    earth shall do the same;
Holy is the Lord and mighty
    is His name.

16. If You'll Take My Jesus

If you'll take my Jesus while
    He's passing by;
If you'll take my Jesus He'll
    hear your heart's cry;
If you'll take my Jesus He'll
    surely satisfy;
If you'll take my Jesus today.

17. I Know The Lord Will Make A Way*

I know the Lord will make a
    way for me,
I know the Lord will make a
    way for me,
If I live a holy life, shun the
    wrong and do the right,
I know the Lord will make a
    way for me.

18. I'll Live For Him

I'll live for Him who died
    for me,
How happy then my life will
    be;
I'll live for Him who died for
    me,
My Savior and my God!

19. I Love Him

I love Him, I love him,
    Because He first loved me,
And purchased my salvation,
    On Calvary's tree.

20. I Love Him For He Is Mine*

I love Him for He is Mine;
I love Him for He is divine;
I'll love him forever it seems;
This Jesus, the Nazarene.

21. I'm So Glad Jesus Lifted Me*

I'm so glad Jesus lifted me,
I'm so glad Jesus lifted me,
I'm so glad Jesus lifted me,
Singing glory, Hallelujah,
    Jesus Lifted me.

22. I Need Thee

I need Thee, Oh, I need Thee,
Every hour I need Thee,
O Bless me now my Savior,
I come to Thee.

23. I See A Crimson Stream

I see a crimson stream
    of blood,
It flows from Calvary,
Its waves which reach the
    throne of God,
Are sweeping over me.

24. It Shall Flow Like A River*

It shall flow like a river, it
    shall fall like the rain,
It shall rise as the dawning in
    the glory o'er the land,
For the knowledge of the Lord
    shall fill all the earth,
And the Spirit of the Lord
    shall fall.

25. It's Real*

It's real, it's real, I know it's
    real;
This Pentecostal blessing, Oh,
    I know, I know it's real.
It's real, it's real, I know it's
    real;
This Pentecostal blessing, Oh,
    I know, I know it's real.

26. I've Got Peace Like A River

I've got peace like a river,
Peace like a river,
I've got peace like a river,
in my soul;
I've got peace like a river,
Peace like a river,
I've got peace like a river
in my soul.

27. I Will Praise Him

I will praise Him! I will
praise Him!
Praise the Lamb for sinners
slain;
Give Him glory, all ye people,
For His blood can wash away
each stain.

28. I Will Sing Of The Mercies

I will sing of the mercies of
the Lord forever,
I will sing, I will sing;
I will sing of the mercies of
the Lord forever,
I will sing of the mercies of
the Lord.

With my mouth will I make
known,
Thy faithfulness, Thy
faithfulness.
With my mouth will I make
known,
Thy faithfulness to all
generations.
(Repeat first verse)

29. Jesus Breaks Every Fetter*

Jesus breaks every fetter,
Jesus breaks every fetter,
Jesus breaks every fetter,
And He sets me free.

30. Jesus Is The One*

Jesus is the One, yes he's the
only One;
Let Him have His way until
the day is done.
When He speaks you know,
dark clouds will have to go,
Just because He loves you so.

31. Jesus Is The Sweetest Name

Jesus is the sweetest name I
know,
And He's just the same, as
His lovely name,
That's the reason why I love
Him so;
For Jesus is the sweetest
name I know.

32. Jesus, Jesus, Jesus*

Jesus, Jesus, Jesus,
Never Have I heard a name,
That thrills my soul like Thine
Jesus, Jesus, Jesus
Oh what wondrous grace
That links that lovely name
with mine.

33. Jesus Use Me*

Jesus, use me, and O lord,
don't refuse me,
For surely there's a work that
I can do:
And even tho' it's humble,
Help my will to crumble,
Tho' the cost be great, I'll
work for you.

34. Just To Have A Touch, Lord From You*

Just to have a touch, Lord
from you,
To help with the trials I go
thru;
Tho' dark may be the night, it
brings a ray of light, when
I have a touch,
Lord, from you.

35. My Burdens Rolled Away

Rolled away, rolled away,
rolled away;
Every burden of my heart
rolled away.
Rolled away, rolled away,
rolled away;
Every burden of my heart
rolled away.
Every sin had to go, 'neath
the crimson flow,
hallelujah,
Rolled away, rolled away,
rolled away;
Every burden of my heart
rolled away.

36. My Jesus, I Love Thee*

My Jesus, I love Thee, I love
Thee, I do;
My Jesus, I love Thee, I love
Thee, I do;
Thy beauty enthralls me, Thy
love has filled my soul;
My Jesus, I love Thee, I love
Thee, I do.

37. Near The Cross

Jesus, keep me near the
cross,
There a precious fountain
Free to all a healing stream,
Flows from Calvary's
mountain.
In the cross, in the cross,
be my glory ever;
'Til my raptured soul shall
find
Rest beyond the river.

38. Never Failed Me Yet

Never failed me yet, never
failed me yet,
Jesus' love never failed
me yet;
This one thing I know, that
where-e'er I go,
Jesus' love has never failed me
yet.

39. Not By Might

Not by might; not by pow'r;
by my Spirit, saith the
Lord of Hosts;
Not by might; not by pow'r;
By my Spirit, saith
the Lord;
This mountain shall
be removed,
This mountain shall
be removed,
This mountain shall
be removed.
By my Spirit, saith the Lord.

40. Oh, Glory, Glory, Glory*

On Sunday I am happy; on
Monday, full of joy;
On Tuesday, I have peace
within that nothing can
destroy;
On Wednesday and on
Thurday I'm walking in
the light;
Friday is a heaven to me;
and Saturday's always
bright.

Oh, Glory, glory, glory,
Oh glory to the Lamb,
Hallelujah I am saved
And bound for the happy land.

41. Oh, How I Love Jesus*

Oh, how I love Jesus,
Oh, how I love Jesus,
Oh, how I love Jesus,
Because He first loved me.

42. Oh, It Is Jesus*

Oh, it is Jesus, Yes, it
is Jesus;
Oh, it is Jesus in my soul,
For I have touched the hem of
His garment,
And His blood has made me
whole.

43. Oh, I Want To See Him

Oh, I want to see Him, look
upon His face,
There to sing forever of His
saving grace;
On the streets of Glory let me
lift my voice;
Cares all past, home at last,
ever to rejoice.

44. Oh, Say But I'm Glad

Oh, say but I'm glad,
I'm glad;
Oh, say but I'm glad.
Jesus has come and my cup's
over-run,
Oh, say but I'm glad.

45. Oh, The Blood Of Jesus*

Oh, the blood of Jesus,
Oh, the blood of Jesus,
Oh, the blood of Jesus,
It washes white as snow.

46. Praise Him*

Praise Him, Praise Him,
Praise Him in the morning,
praise Him in the
noontime,
Praise Him, Praise Him
Praise Him when the sun
goes down.

47. Reach Out And Touch The Lord

Reach out and touch the Lord
as He walks by;

You'll find he's not too busy
to hear your cry.
He's passing by this moment,
your needs He'll supply;
Reach out and touch the Lord
as He walks by.

48. **Revive Us Again**

Hallelujah, Thine the
Glory (Chorus)
Hallelujah, Amen
Hallelujah, Thine the Glory,
Revive us Again.

We praise Thee oh God, (vs. 1)
For the Son of Thy love,
For Jesus who died and is
now gone above.

Revive us again   (vs. 2)
Fill each heart with Thy love,
May each soul be rekindled
with fire from above.

49. **Souls, Lord***

Souls, Lord; souls, Lord;
Give me a passion for souls,
I pray.
Help me to open this mouth
of mine
To tell of your wonderful
Love divine.
Souls, Lord: souls, Lord;
Help me to win them for Thee
Help me to be a witness for
Thee;
Give me a passion for souls.

50. **Stop And Let Me Tell You***

Stop! and let me tell you
What the good Lord's done
for me;
Stop! and let me tell you
How the good Lord set
me free
For He has healed my body
and saved my soul,
Baptized me and made me
whole
Stop! and let me tell you
What the good Lord's done
for me.

51. **Sunlight**

Sunlight, sunlight in my soul
today;
Sunlight, sunlight all along
the way;
Since the Savior found me;
took away my sin,
I have had the sunlight of His
love within.

52. **Sweep Over my Soul***

Sweep over my soul, Sweep
over my soul.
Sweet Spirit, sweep over my
soul.
My rest is complete; When I
sit at His feet;
Sweet Spirit; sweep over my
soul.

53. **Sweet Jesus***

Sweet Jesus, sweet Jesus,
What a wonder you are,
You're brighter than the
morning star;
You're fairer, much fairer,
Than the lily that grows by
the way side,
Precious, more precious
than gold.
You're like the rose of Sharon,
You're the fairest of the fair,
You are all my heart could
e'er desire;
Sweet Jesus, sweet Jesus,
What a wonder you are,
You're precious,
more precious than gold.

54. **Take The Name Of Jesus
With You**

Precious name, oh how sweet;
Hope of earth, and joy of
heaven;
Precious name, oh how sweet;
Hope of earth, and joy of
heaven.

55. **The Deaf Shall Know**

The deaf shall know, Him
whom to know is life.
The deaf shall know, the
Savior, Jesus Christ;
The deaf shall know, the life,
the truth, the way
The deaf shall know that
Jesus came to save.

56. **The Lion Of Judah***

The Lion of Judah shall break
every chain,
And give to us the victory
again and again.
The Lion of Judah shall break
every chain,
And give to us the victory
again and again.

The Lord is returning, oh,
  shout, "Hallelujah,"
Our blessed Redeemer is
  coming again;
For soon we shall see Him,
  the King in His beauty
The joyful shouts will then
  ring out "He comes
  to reign."

57. The Name Of Jesus

"Jesus" oh, how sweet
  the name!
"Jesus" every day the same;
"Jesus" let all saints
  proclaim
Thy worthy praise forever.

58. There Is Power In The Blood

There is pow'r, pow'r,
  Wonder-working pow'r,
In the blood of the Lamb;
There is pow'r, pow'r,
  Wonder-working pow'r,
In the precious blood of the
  Lamb.

59. To Be Like Jesus*

To be like Jesus, to be like
  Jesus,
All I ask to be like Him.
All through life's journey,
  from earth to glory,
All I ask to be like him.

60. To God Be The Glory

Praise the Lord, praise the
  Lord
Let the earth hear His voice;
Praise the Lord, praise the
  Lord
Let the people rejoice;
Oh, come to the Father, thro'
  Jesus the Son
And give Him the glory; great
  things He hath done.

61. Trust In The Lord

Trust in the Lord and don't
  despair,
He is a Friend so true;
No matter what your troubles
  are,
Jesus will see you through.
Sing, sing, when the day is
  bright,
Sing, sing, through the
  darkest night
Every day, all the way,
Let us sing, sing, sing!

62. Victory

Hallelujah, what a thought!
Jesus full salvation brought,
Victory, victory.
Let the powers of sin assail,
Heaven's grace can never fail,
Victory, victory.
Victory, yes, victory;
Hallelujah! I am free, Jesus
  gives me victory.
Glory, glory, Hallelujah!
He is all in all to me.

63. Walking With The King*

Hallelujah, I'm walking with
  the King,
Praise His holy name,
Walking with the King,
Hallelujah, I'm walking with
  the King,
Every day I'm walking with
  the King!

64. We'll Give The Glory To Jesus*

We'll give the glory to Jesus,
And tell of His love,
And tell of His love;
We'll give the glory to Jesus,
And tell of His wonderful
  love.

65. What The World Needs Is Jesus*

What the world needs is Jesus
Just a glimpse of Him;
What the world needs is Jesus
Just a glimpse of Him;
He will bring joy and
  gladness,
Take away sin and sadness;
What the world needs is Jesus
Just a glimpse of Him.

66. When Jesus Breaks The Morning*

When Jesus breaks the
  morning,
The hosts of heav'n will sing,
"hosanna in the highest,"
He is our conq'ring King.
We'll clasp our hands,
  together
Around the heav'nly throne,
And join the angels singing:
At last, at last, we're home.

Scriptures
to practice in the American Standard Version

1. In the beginning was the Word, and the Word was with God, and the Word was God (John 1:1).

2. The same was in the beginning with God. All things were made through him; and without him was not anything made that hath been made (John 1:2, 3).

3. In him was life; and the life was the light of men. And the light shineth in darkness; and the darkness apprehended [overcame] it not (John 1:4, 5).

4. There came a man, sent from God, whose name was John. The same came for witness, that he might bear witness of the light, that all might [can, trust] believe through him (John 1:6, 7).

5. He was in the world, and the world was made through him, and the world knew him not. He came unto his own, and they that were his own received him not (John 1:10, 11).

6. But as many received him, to them gave he the right to become children of God, **even** to them that believe on his name (John 1:12).

7. John beareth witness of him, and crieth, saying, This was he of whom I said, he that cometh after me is become before me: for he was before [in time] me. For of his fulness we all received, and grade for grace. For the law was given through Moses; grace and truth came through Jesus Christ (John 1:15 - 17).

8. John answered them, saying, I baptize in water: in the midst of you standeth one whom ye know not, **even** he that cometh after me, the latchet of whose shoe I am not worthy to unloose (John 1:26, 27).

9. And the third day there was a marriage in Cana of Galilee; and the mother of Jesus was there: and Jesus also was bidden, and his disciples, to the marriage (John 2:1,2).

10. And when the wine failed, the mother of Jesus saith unto him, They have no wine. And Jesus saith unto her, Woman, what have I to do with thee? mine hour is not yet come. His mother saith unto the servants, Whatsoever he saith unto you, do it (John 2:3 - 5).

11. Jesus answered, Verily, verily, I say unto thee, Except one be born of water and the Spirit, he cannot enter into the kingdom of God. That which is born of the flesh is flesh; and that which is born of the Spirit is spirit (John 3:5, 6).

12. He that believeth on the Son hath eternal life; but he that obeyeth not the Son shall not see life, but the wrath of God abideth on him (John 3:36).

13. For God so loved the world, that he gave his only begotten Son, that whosoever believeth on him should not perish, but have eternal life. For God sent not his Son into the world to judge the world; but that the world should be saved through him (John 3:16, 17).

14. He that believeth on him is not judged: he that believeth not hath been judged already, because he hath not believed on the name of the only begotten Son of God. And this is the judgment, that the light is come into the world, and men loved the darkness rather than the light; for their works were evil (John 3:18,19).

15. He that cometh from above is above all: he that is of the earth is of the earth, and of the earth he speaketh; he that cometh from heaven is above all (John 3:31).

16. Behold, I stand at the door and knock: if any man hear my my voice and open the door, I will come in to him, and will sup with him, and he with me (Revelation 3:20).

17. But whosoever drinketh of the water that I shall give him shall never thirst; but the water that I shall give him shall become in him a well of water springing up unto eternal life (John 4:14).

18. But the hour cometh, and now is, when the true worshippers shall worship the Father in spirit and truth: for such doth the Father seek to be his worshippers. God is a Spirit: and they that worship him must worship in spirit and truth (John 4:23, 24).

19. Say not ye, There are yet four months, and **then** cometh the harvest? behold, I say unto you, Lift up your eyes, and look on the fields that they are white already unto harvest (John 4:34).

20. Verily, verily, I say unto you, He that heareth my word, and believeth him that sent me, hath eternal life, and cometh not into judgment, but hath passed out of death into life (John 5:24).

21. For God my witness, whom I serve in my spirit in the gospel of his Son, how unceasingly I make mention of you, always in my prayers making request, if by any means now at length I may be prospered by the will of God to come unto you (Romans 1: 9, 10).

22. I beseech you therefore, brethren, by the mercies of God, to present your bodies a living sacrifice, holy, acceptable to God, **which is** your spiritual service (Romans 12:1).

23. I will give thanks unto Jehovah with my whole heart; I will show forth all thy marvelous works. I will be glad and exult in thee; I will sing praise to thy name, O thou Most High (Psalm 9:1, 2).

24. Remember also thy Creator in the days of thy youth, before the evil days come, and the years draw nigh, when thou shalt say, I have no pleasure in them (Ecclesiastes 12:1).

25. In the year that king Uzziah died I saw the Lord sitting upon a throne, high and lifted up; and his train filled the temple (Isaiah 6:1).

26. Ho, every one that thirsteth, come ye to the waters, and he that hath no money; come ye, buy, and eat; yea, come, buy wine and milk without money and without price (Isaiah 55:1).

27. Because if thou shalt confess with thy mouth Jesus as Lord, and shalt believe in thy heart that God raised him from the dead, thou shalt be saved; for with the heart man believeth unto righteousness; and with the mouth confession is made unto salvation (Romans 10:9, 10).

28. If we confess our sins, he is faithful and righteous to forgive us our sins, and to cleanse us from all unrighteousness (John 1:9).

29. For all have sinned, and fall short of the glory of God. For the wages of sin is death; but the free gift of God is eternal life in Christ Jesus our Lord (Romans 3:23; 6:23).

30. And if any man shall take away from the words of the book of this prophecy, God shall take away his part from the tree of life, and out of the holy city, which are written in this book. He who testifiedth these things saith, Yea: I come quickly. Amen: come, Lord Jesus (Revelation 22:19, 20).

Index
First occurence of each word only·

230

232

236

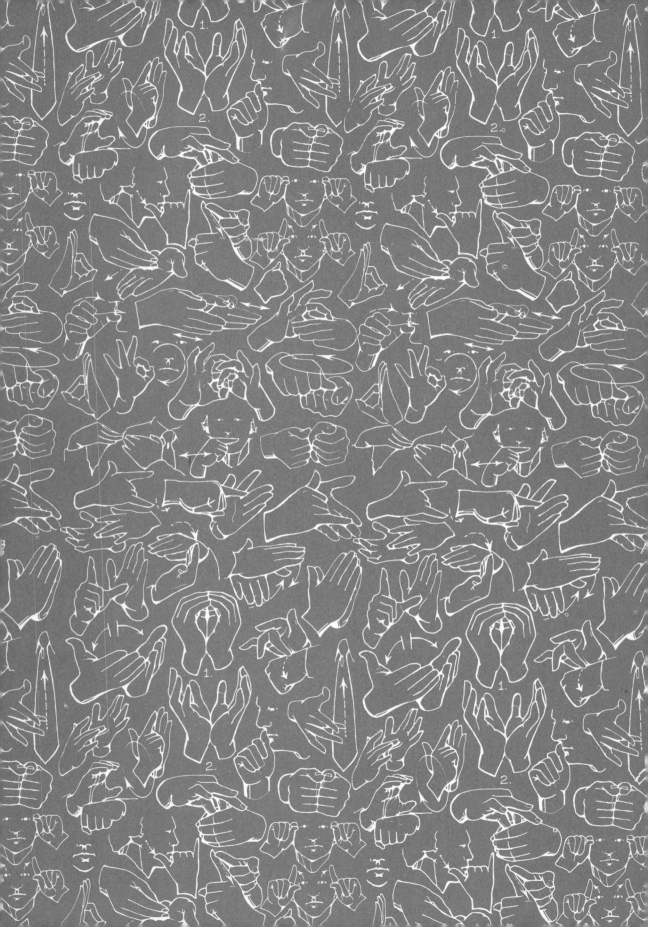